ideals

Cookie
COOKBOOK
by Darlene Kronschnabel

What absolute delight to have more than two hundred cookie recipes in one collection . . . to page through, glancing at the beautiful pictures, enjoying the artwork and illustrations, and reading the recipes . . . trying to decide which cookie recipe to try first!

. . . and to know that no matter which recipe is selected . . . the old-time favorite, the exotic new, the very special one . . . pressed, refrigerated or baked . . . that the cookie will be an instant success!

We just know that you will thoroughly enjoy THE *ideals* COOKIE COOKBOOK . . . filled with useful baking tips and fascinating anecdotes of cookie lore . . . as well as a little bit of poetry and prose and a touch of photography and art . . . to make this a cookbook of sugar and spice and everything nice!

. . . a cookie cookbook that is certain to please you, your family, and your friends.

Darlene Kronschnabel
author

An *ideals* Publication
Third Printing
ISBN 0-89542-639-0 295
IDEALS PUBLISHING CORP., MILWAUKEE, WIS. 53201

CONTENTS

Editorial Director, James Kuse
Managing Editor, Ralph Luedtke
Production Editor/Manager, Richard Lawson
Photographic Editor, Gerald Koser

designed by
Carol McAvoy

Pictured opposite
Three-Way Peanut Butter Cookies, page 4

ALL-AMERICAN COOKIES

THREE-WAY PEANUT BUTTER COOKIES

½ c. butter
⅓ c. peanut butter
½ c. sugar
¼ c. brown sugar
1 egg
2 T. milk
1 t. vanilla
2¼ c. flour
¼ t. baking powder
¼ t. salt
2 1-oz. squares unsweetened chocolate, melted
Salted peanuts, chopped
Semisweet chocolate chips

Cream butter and peanut butter. Gradually add sugars, beating until light and fluffy. Add egg, milk and vanilla; beat well. Combine flour, baking powder and salt; gradually blend into creamed mixture. Divide dough into two parts, one slightly larger than the other. Add cooled chocolate to the smaller portion. Mix until evenly blended.

LAYER BARS

Divide chocolate dough in half; repeat for peanut butter dough. Roll out each dough between 2 sheets of waxed paper to form an 8-inch square. Invert one square of peanut butter dough on top of one square of chocolate dough, removing waxed paper. Invert remaining chocolate dough on top, then remaining peanut butter dough, to form four layers. Cover and chill several hours or overnight. Cut into thirty-two 2-inch bars. Place on cookie sheets. Bake in 350° oven 12 to 14 minutes. Drizzle with melted chocolate chips if desired. Makes 32 bars.

PINWHEEL LOLLIPOPS

Roll out each half of dough between two sheets of waxed paper to form a 14 x 8-inch rectangle. Invert chocolate dough on top of peanut butter dough, removing waxed paper. Roll up along 14-inch side as for jelly roll. Cover and chill several hours or overnight. Cut into ¼-inch slices. Place 5-inch wooden sticks or skewers on cookie sheets. Press one cookie on end of each stick to form lollipops. Bake in 350° oven 10 to 12 minutes. Makes 56 lollipops.

TWO-TONE COOKIES

Roll out peanut butter dough between two sheets of waxed paper to form a 14 x 6-inch rectangle. Shape chocolate dough to form a 14-inch log. Roll up peanut butter dough around chocolate log, removing paper. Cover and chill several hours or overnight. Cut into ¼-inch slices. Sprinkle with chopped peanuts, packing lightly. Place on cookie sheets. Bake in 350° oven 10 to 12 minutes. Makes 56 cookies.

> Don't bake cookies too long; they will become hard.

OLD-FASHIONED GINGERSNAPS

2¼ c. flour
½ t. cinnamon
1 t. ginger
¼ t. salt
⅓ c. shortening
¾ c. sugar
1 egg, well beaten
½ c. light molasses
2 t. baking soda
2 t. hot water

Sift flour, cinnamon, ginger and salt. Set aside. Cream shortening and sugar until light. Add egg and molasses. Dissolve soda in hot water; add to creamed mixture. Stir in dry ingredients. Chill for ease in handling. Roll out on a lightly floured board to ⅛-inch thickness and cut with a 2-inch round cookie cutter. Place on greased baking sheet. Bake in 350° oven 10 to 12 minutes. For a crackled surface, brush each cookie with water before baking. Makes about 6 dozen cookies.

THE WORLD'S GREATEST COOKIE

1 c. butter or margarine
1 c. crunchy peanut butter
1 c. sugar
1 c. brown sugar
2 eggs
2 c. flour
1 t. baking soda
1 6-oz. pkg. semisweet chocolate chips

Cream butter and peanut butter. Gradually add sugars and cream until blended. Add eggs, one at a time, and beat until smooth. Sift together flour and soda and add to creamed mixture. Stir in chocolate chips. Drop from a teaspoon onto a greased baking sheet. Slightly flatten cookie dough with back of spoon. Bake in 325° oven for 15 minutes. Makes 6 dozen 2-inch cookies.

Hermits are traditionally spicy rich and plump with raisins. As the recipe originated in Cape Cod, it is not surprising they went to sea on Clipper Ships. Records show that hermits were still seafarers in World War II. A recipe for hermits was found posted in the galley of the USS *North Carolina*, now a state memorial anchored at Wilmington, North Carolina.

CINNAMON HERMITS

3½ c. flour
4½ t. baking powder
1½ t. salt
2 c. light brown sugar
½ c. shortening
1½ t. cinnamon
½ t. cloves
3 large eggs
2 T. milk
2 c. raisins

Sift together the first 3 ingredients and set aside. Cream sugar, shortening and spices. Beat in eggs. Blend in milk and raisins. Gradually stir in sifted flour mixture. Drop from a teaspoon onto lightly greased cookie sheet. Bake in a 375° oven 15 to 18 minutes. Makes 6 dozen cookies.

DOUBLE CHOCOLATE CHIP COOKIES

2½ c. flour
1 T. baking powder
1 t. baking soda
1 t. salt
1 c. butter, softened
¾ c. sugar
½ c. light brown sugar
2 eggs
1 t. vanilla
3 1-oz. squares unsweetened chocolate, melted
1 6-oz. pkg. semisweet chocolate chips

Sift together flour, baking powder, soda and salt. Cream butter and sugars until fluffy. Add eggs and vanilla; beat well. Stir in chocolate. Add flour mixture and blend until smooth. Fold in chocolate chips. Drop by rounded teaspoons onto lightly greased baking sheets. Bake in 350° oven 10 to 12 minutes. Remove from baking sheets and cool on wire racks. Makes about 6½ dozen.

GRANDMA'S COOKIE JAR

When I went to visit Grandma
I was always thrilled
For I knew she kept
A cookie jar well filled.

Quickly I removed my wraps
And Grandma led the way
Into a pungent kitchen
With treasures on display.

Peanut butter cookies,
Gumdrops tart and sweet,
Macaroons and gingersnaps
And brownies for a treat.

With a glass of buttermilk
I tasted everything,
With Grandma looking on at me
As though I were a king.

I love to visit Grandma;
It's a trip I most enjoy,
Though manhood's now replaced
That eager little boy.

Bernice Peers

PUMPKIN COOKIE FACES

¼ c. shortening
⅔ c. brown sugar
½ c. mashed pumpkin
¾ c. light molasses
3 c. flour
1 t. baking soda
½ t. salt
½ t. ginger
½ t. cinnamon
½ t. nutmeg
½ t. allspice
   Icing, raisins, gumdrops and other candies

Cream sugar and shortening; stir in pumpkin and molasses. Sift together flour, soda, salt and spices; blend into pumpkin mixture. Cover and chill 2 to 3 hours. Roll dough ¼ inch thick on lightly floured board. Cut with floured pumpkin-shaped cookie cutter. Gently place on lightly greased baking sheets; bake at 375° for 8 to 10 minutes. Cool. Decorate with icing, raisins and candies. Makes 2 dozen 3-inch cookies.

OLD-FASHIONED OATMEAL COOKIES

1 c. butter
1½ c. brown sugar
2 eggs
2 c. flour
2 t. baking powder
¼ t. baking soda
1 t. salt
1 t. cinnamon
1 t. nutmeg
½ c. milk
2 c. uncooked oats
2 c. raisins
½ c. chopped walnuts

Cream butter and sugar until light and fluffy. Add eggs; mix well. Combine flour, baking powder, soda, salt and spices. Add to creamed mixture alternately with milk. Stir in oats, raisins and nuts. Drop by heaping teaspoons onto buttered cookie sheets. Bake at 375° for 9 to 11 minutes or until set. Makes about 8 dozen.

Each Colonial homemaker had her own favorite recipe for jumbles, or jumbals. These early cookies, or biscuits as they were known, received their name from the method of mixing.

In the days before accurate measurements, cooks added a pinch of salt, lard the size of an egg, a handful of flour and "jumbled" the mixture together. Hence the name.

OLD-FASHIONED CINNAMON JUMBLES

2 c. flour
½ t. baking soda
½ t. salt
½ c. butter, softened
1¼ c. sugar
1 egg
¾ c. buttermilk
1 t. vanilla
1 t. cinnamon

Sift together flour, baking soda and salt. Set aside. Cream butter, 1 cup sugar and egg until light and fluffy. Blend in buttermilk and vanilla. Stir in dry ingredients. Mix well. Chill dough. Drop by rounded teaspoons 2 inches apart on greased baking sheets. Sprinkle with remaining sugar mixed with cinnamon. Bake in 400° oven 8 to 10 minutes until set but not brown. Makes 4 dozen 2 inch cookies.

PEANUT BUTTER CRISPIES

2½ c. self-rising flour
½ c. butter, softened
1 c. chunky peanut butter
1 c. brown sugar
⅓ c. water

Cream butter, peanut butter, and sugar until smooth. Add flour alternately with water, mixing well after each addition. Shape into two rolls, 2 inches in diameter. Chill several hours or overnight. Slice ¼-inch thick. Place on ungreased baking sheet and bake in 400° oven 8 to 10 minutes. Makes 3½ dozen cookies.

Pictured opposite
Pumpkin Cookie Faces

BAR COOKIES

ROCKY ROAD BARS

¼ c. flour
¼ t. baking powder
⅛ t. salt
⅓ c. brown sugar
 1 egg
 1 T. butter
½ t. vanilla
½ c. finely chopped walnuts
  Rocky Road Topping

Sift flour, baking powder and salt. Add remaining ingredients except walnuts, and beat until smooth. Stir in walnuts. Turn into greased 9-inch square pan. Bake at 350° for 15 minutes, or just until top is lightly browned and springs back when touched lightly. Remove from oven and immediately cover with Rocky Road Topping. Return pan to oven for 2 minutes only, just until chocolate is softened. Remove from oven and swirl chocolate over marshmallows and walnuts. Cool until chocolate is set before cutting. Makes fifteen 1¾ x 3-inch bars.

ROCKY ROAD TOPPING

 1 c. miniature marshmallows
½ c. chopped walnuts
 1 6-oz pkg. semisweet chocolate chips

Place ingredients in order listed over the baked layer.

> To store bar cookies, do not cut into bars but wrap entire square in foil and store in cool place. To remove from pan without cutting, line the bottom and two sides of the pan with foil before baking. Grease pan. Grease foil. When square has cooled, loosen sides and lift out, using foil as handles.

MARY'S MARBLE SQUARES

½ c. butter or margarine
¼ c. + 2 T. sugar
¼ c. + 2 T. brown sugar
 1 t. vanilla
 1 egg
 1 c. flour
½ t. baking soda
½ t. salt
½ c. sunflower seeds or coarsely chopped walnuts
 1 6-oz. pkg. semisweet chocolate chips

Cream butter, sugars, and vanilla. Beat in egg. Sift together flour, soda and salt and blend into creamed mixture. Stir in sunflower seeds or nuts. Spread in greased and floured 13 x 9 x 2-inch pan. Sprinkle chocolate chips over top. Place in preheated 375° oven 1 minute. Remove from oven and run knife through dough to marbleize. Return to oven and bake 12 to 15 minutes or until golden brown. Remove from oven and cool. Cut into 2-inch squares. Makes 2 dozen bars.

BUTTERSCOTCH-COFFEE-SPICE BARS

 1 c. brown sugar
½ c. shortening
 1 egg
½ c. hot water
 1 t. instant coffee
1½ c. flour
 1 t. baking powder
½ t. baking soda
½ t. salt
½ t. cinnamon
 1 c. butterscotch chips
½ c. chopped nuts

Combine sugar, shortening and egg; beat until creamy. Mix hot water and instant coffee; blend into creamed mixture. Sift together flour, baking powder, soda, salt and cinnamon; gradually stir into creamed mixture. Add butterscotch chips and chopped nuts; mix well. Spread in greased and floured 13 x 9 x 2-inch pan. Bake in 350° oven about 20 to 25 minutes. Cool. Cut into 3 x 1½-inch bars. Makes 2 dozen bars.

CALIFORNIA DREAM BARS

CRUST

½ c. brown sugar
1 c. flour
½ c. butter, melted

Combine ingredients. Press firmly into bottom and sides of an ungreased 7 x 11 x 2-inch pan. Bake at 375° about 15 minutes. Remove from oven. Add topping.

TOPPING

2 eggs, slightly beaten
1 c. brown sugar
1 c. nuts, coarsely chopped
1 c. flaked coconut
2 T. flour
½ t. baking powder
¼ t. salt

Combine ingredients, blending well. Spread over baked crust. Return to oven. Bake at 375° for 15 minutes longer. Remove from oven and cool. Cut into bars or squares. Makes about 30.

BUTTERSCOTCH-SUNFLOWER NUT BARS

1 c. butter
1½ c. brown sugar
½ c. granulated sugar
3 eggs, separated
1 t. vanilla
2 c. flour
1 6-oz. pkg. butterscotch chips
¾ c. salted sunflower nuts

Cream butter with granulated sugar and ½ cup brown sugar until smooth. Add well-beaten egg yolks and mix well. Add vanilla and flour and blend well. Press into a greased jelly roll pan or 10 x 15-inch cookie sheet. Sprinkle butterscotch chips over top. Beat egg whites until stiff. Fold in remaining brown sugar. Spread mixture over crust and chips. Sprinkle sunflower nuts over the top. Bake in a 350° oven for 25 minutes or until lightly browned. Cool and cut into 3 dozen bars. For variation, use chocolate chips and salted peanuts.

SPICY JUMBO BARS

3 c. flour
1 t. baking soda
½ t. salt
1 t. cinnamon
½ t. nutmeg
1 c. brown sugar
1 c. granulated sugar
¾ c. butter, softened
1 egg
3 t. vanilla
½ c. sour cream
1 6-oz. pkg. semisweet chocolate chips
1½ c. raisins
½ c. chopped nuts

Sift together flour, soda, salt and spices. Set aside. Cream sugars and butter. Add egg and vanilla, mixing thoroughly. Alternately add dry ingredients and sour cream to creamed mixture. Stir in raisins, chips and nuts. Spread in a 15 x 10-inch pan lined with waxed paper. Chill at least 3 hours in refrigerator or 1 hour in freezer. Invert pan and remove chilled cookie dough. Peel off waxed paper and cut into 2 x 1½-inch rectangles. Place 2 inches apart on ungreased baking sheet. Bake at 400° for 10 to 12 minutes. Remove from baking sheet and cool on rack. Makes 50 bars.

COCONUT MOUNDS

16 graham crackers, finely crushed
⅓ c. butter
2 T. confectioners' sugar
1 17-oz. can flaked coconut
1 14-oz. can sweetened condensed milk
1 12-oz. pkg. semisweet chocolate chips
2 T. butter

Combine graham cracker crumbs, ⅓ cup butter, and sugar. Pat mixture into a greased 13 x 9-inch pan. Bake at 350° for 5 minutes. Remove from oven. Stir together coconut and milk. Pour over crust. Return pan to oven and continue to bake at 350° for 15 minutes. Remove from oven and cool for 5 minutes. Melt chocolate chips with remaining butter over low heat. Pour melted mixture over all. Allow to cool before cutting into slender bars.

Lemon Cheese Balls
Rich Butter Cookies

RICH BUTTER COOKIES

¾ c. butter	½ t. vanilla
½ c. sugar	½ t. almond or
1 egg	lemon extract
2¼ c. flour	1⅓ c. flaked coconut

Cream butter and sugar until fluffy. Add egg and beat well. Add flour, a small amount at a time, mixing thoroughly after each addition. Blend in vanilla, almond extract and coconut. Divide dough in two portions and wrap each in waxed paper. Chill 30 minutes.

Roll chilled dough ⅛ inch thick. Cut into shapes with lightly floured 2-inch cookie cutters. Bake on ungreased baking sheets at 400° for about 6 minutes, or until edges just begin to brown. Makes about 5 dozen cookies.

BUTTER AND DAIRY COOKIES

TWO-WAY BUTTER COOKIES

BASIC DOUGH

1 c. butter
1½ c. confectioners' sugar
1 egg
1 t. vanilla
2½ c. flour
1 t. baking soda
1 t. cream of tartar
¼ t. salt

Cream butter and sugar until fluffy. Beat in egg and vanilla. Sift together flour, soda, cream of tartar and salt. Gradually add to creamed mixture. Use half of dough for Butter Fingers and half for Molasses Spice-Eez.

BUTTER FINGERS

½ Basic Dough
½ c. nuts, chopped
¼ c. candied cherries, chopped

Add nuts and cherries to dough. Chill 30 minutes. Shape into oblongs the size of a little finger. Place on ungreased baking sheets. Bake in 400° oven 7 to 8 minutes. Remove to wire rack to cool. Makes 3 dozen.

MOLASSES SPICE-EEZ

½ Basic Dough
2 T. molasses
1 t. cinnamon
½ t. ginger
¼ t. nutmeg

Combine all ingredients. Chill at least 30 minutes. On floured surface, roll dough to ⅛-inch thickness; cut into desired shapes. Place on ungreased baking sheets. Bake in 400° oven 5 to 6 minutes. Remove to wire rack to cool. Makes 4 dozen.

SOUR CREAM ORANGE COOKIES

½ c. butter
1½ c. brown sugar
2 eggs
1 t. vanilla
1 t. baking soda
2¼ c. flour
1 t. salt
1 c. sour cream
1 c. chopped walnuts
Creamy Orange Frosting

Cream butter and sugar; add eggs and vanilla. Alternately add sifted dry ingredients with sour cream, beginning and ending with dry ingredients. Blend well. Stir in nuts. Drop from teaspoon onto greased cookie sheets. Bake at 350° for 10 to 12 minutes. While warm, frost with Creamy Orange Frosting. Makes 6 dozen cookies.

CREAMY ORANGE FROSTING

2 c. confectioners' sugar
1 t. vanilla
2 T. butter
1 t. grated orange rind
1 to 3 T. orange juice

Combine confectioners' sugar, vanilla, butter and orange rind. Blend in orange juice to spreading consistency.

LEMON CHEESE BALLS

½ c. butter
1 3-oz. pkg. cream cheese, softened
½ c. sugar
1 T. grated lemon rind
½ t. lemon extract
1 c. flour
1 t. baking powder
¼ t. salt
1¾ c. cornflakes, coarsely crushed

Cream butter and cream cheese; add sugar gradually. Add rind and extract. Sift together flour, baking powder and salt and add to mixture. Chill several hours. Shape rounded teaspoons of dough into balls. Roll in cornflake crumbs. Place on ungreased cookie sheet. Bake at 350° about 12 minutes. Makes about 3 dozen cookies.

PRESSED COOKIES

FENNEL COOKIES

1 c. butter
½ c. sugar
1 egg, well beaten
2½ c. flour
½ t. baking powder
1 t. vanilla
1 t. fennel seed

Cream butter and sugar until fluffy. Add egg gradually, beating thoroughly. Stir in flour and baking powder. Blend in vanilla and fennel seed. Force through a cookie press. Bake on ungreased cookie sheet at 350° for 12 minutes. About 5 dozen cookies.

> Don't place dropped cookies too close together on baking sheet. Allow them room to spread.

CREAM CHEESE SPRITZ

½ c. butter
1 3-oz. pkg. cream cheese
⅓ c. sugar
1 egg yolk
1½ t. orange extract
1½ c. flour
½ t. salt
Food colors and decorators

Cream together butter and cheese until soft. Add sugar gradually and mix until light and fluffy. Add egg yolk and orange extract. Stir in flour and salt. Color dough as desired with food coloring. Force dough through a cookie press onto ungreased cookie sheets. Sprinkle with decorators. Bake at 375° for about 10 minutes. Do not overbake. Makes about 4 dozen.

SPRITZ

1 c. butter
½ c. plus 1 T. sugar
1 egg
¾ t. salt
1 t. vanilla
½ t. almond extract
2½ c. flour
Colored sugar, candies for decorating

Cream butter and sugar. Blend in egg, salt, extracts and flour. Knead dough in hands until soft and pliable. Force dough through cookie press onto ungreased cookie sheets. Decorate as desired. Bake at 400° for 8 to 10 minutes. Makes about 6 dozen cookies.

BROWN SUGAR SPRITZ

1 c. butter
¼ c. sugar
⅓ c. light brown sugar
1 egg yolk
½ t. vanilla
¼ t. salt
¼ t. almond extract
2¼ c. flour

Cream butter with sugars. Add egg yolk, vanilla, salt and almond extract. Beat until fluffy. Blend in flour. Knead dough in hands until it is soft and pliable. Force dough through cookie press onto ungreased cookie sheets. Decorate if desired. Bake at 350° about 8 minutes. Makes about 8 dozen.

NORWEGIAN ALMOND COOKIES

¾ c. butter
½ c. confectioners' sugar
1 c. finely ground almonds
1 t. lemon juice
1 egg
1½ c. flour

Cream together butter and sugar until light and fluffy. Force almonds through a coarse sieve and add to creamed mixture. Add lemon juice and egg, mixing well. Gradually blend in flour. Force cookies through cookie press on ungreased cookie sheets. Bake in 400° oven 7 to 10 minutes. Remove at once to cooling rack. Decorate with frosting, if desired. Makes 5 to 6 dozen.

REFRIGERATOR COOKIES

PECAN REFRIGERATOR COOKIES

1 lb. butter	4 c. flour
1 lb. light brown sugar	1 t. cinnamon
	1 t. baking powder
2 eggs	1 t. salt
2 t. vanilla	1 lb. chopped pecans

Cream butter and sugar together until light and fluffy. Beat in eggs, one at a time. Add vanilla. Sift dry ingredients together and add to butter mixture, mixing thoroughly. Stir in pecans. Chill dough for one to two hours. Divide into 6 portions; shape into rolls about 1¾ inches in diameter. Wrap the rolls in waxed paper and chill overnight or longer. Slice about ¼ inch thick. Bake on greased cookie sheet in 375° oven for 10 minutes or until cookies are delicately browned. Makes 14 dozen.

APPLESAUCE FREEZER COOKIES

1 c. butter
1½ c. brown sugar
1 egg, slightly beaten
4 c. flour
1 t. salt
½ t. baking soda
1 t. cinnamon
¼ t. cloves
1 c. thick applesauce, unsweetened
½ c. chopped walnuts

Cream butter and brown sugar until fluffy. Add egg; blend well. Sift together flour, salt, soda, cinnamon and cloves. Add alternately to the creamed mixture with the applesauce. Add chopped walnuts. Form into 4 rolls, 1½ inches in diameter. Wrap in waxed paper; freeze until firm. Slice thinly. Bake on greased cookie sheets at 375° for 15 minutes. Makes 7 dozen cookies.

CHERRY N' CHOCOLATE COOKIES

1 c. butter
1½ c. sugar
1 egg
2 t. vanilla
2½ c. flour
1½ t. baking powder
¾ t. salt
½ c. candied cherries, diced
⅓ c. chopped walnuts
1 square unsweetened chocolate
Hot milk

Sift together flour, baking powder and salt. Cream butter and sugar gradually. Beat in egg and vanilla. Blend in sifted dry ingredients. Divide dough into 2 equal portions. Mix cherries into one portion, walnuts and melted chocolate into remaining portion. Work dough with hands until pliable. Shape each portion of dough into 2 bars 9 x 1½ inches. Wrap in waxed paper; chill until firm. Cut each bar in half lengthwise; brush cut side of bar with milk. Press one cherry and one chocolate bar together. Press firmly. Wrap in waxed paper. Chill until firm. Cut into ¼-inch slices. Bake at 350° about 10 minutes. Makes about 10 dozen.

ORANGE PEANUT REFRIGERATOR COOKIES

2 c. flour
¼ t. baking soda
¼ t. salt
1 c. butter or margarine
½ c. brown sugar
½ c. sugar
1 egg
3 T. frozen orange juice concentrate
1 T. grated orange rind
½ c. chopped peanuts

Sift together flour, baking soda and salt. Cream butter with sugars; beat in egg. Blend in undiluted orange concentrate, orange rind and dry ingredients. Stir in peanuts. Chill dough. Shape into 2 rolls 2 inches in diameter; wrap in waxed paper. Refrigerate several hours or overnight. Cut into ¼-inch slices. Place on ungreased baking sheet. Bake in 400° oven 10 to 12 minutes or until lightly browned. Makes about 4 dozen.

OATMEAL REFRIGERATOR COOKIES

½ c. peanut butter	1¾ c. flour
½ c. butter	2 t. baking soda
2 c. brown sugar	¾ t. salt
1 t. vanilla	1½ c. uncooked oats
2 eggs	½ c. chopped nuts

Cream together peanut butter and butter. Add sugar gradually and cream together until light and fluffy. Add vanilla and eggs and beat well. Mix in flour, sifted together with soda and salt. Then add oats and nuts. Shape dough into rolls about 2 inches in diameter. Wrap in waxed paper. Chill in refrigerator. Slice ⅛ inch thick. Place on greased cookie sheet and bake in 350° oven for about 15 minutes. Makes 6 to 6½ dozen.

Real vanilla comes from the fruit of a tropical orchid, mostly grown in the Madagascar region.

REFRIGERATOR SANDWICH COOKIES

¾ c. butter	1 egg yolk
¼ c. light brown sugar	1 t. vanilla
	1¾ c. flour
¼ c. sugar	Pecan halves

Cream butter and sugars and beat until blended. Beat in egg and vanilla; gradually add flour. Chill for ease in handling. Form into 2 rolls, each 7 inches long and 1½ inches in diameter. Wrap in waxed paper; chill several hours or overnight. Cut into ⅛-inch slices and place on lightly greased baking sheets. Bake in 350° oven 8 to 10 minutes. Remove to wire rack to cool. Put 2 cookies together with vanilla frosting and top with a dollop of frosting and a pecan half. Makes about 3 dozen.

VANILLA FROSTING

¼ c. butter	1 egg white
2½ c. confectioners' sugar	½ t. vanilla
	Food color

Cream butter. Add sugar alternately with egg white, beating until light and fluffy. Blend in vanilla and food coloring. Makes 1 cup.

ORANGE-COCONUT REFRIGERATOR COOKIES

½ c. butter	
½ c. light brown sugar	
¾ c. sugar	
1 egg	
2 t. grated orange peel	
1 t. vanilla	
1¾ c. flour	
2 t. baking powder	
½ t. salt	
⅓ c. flaked coconut	

Cream butter and sugars. Beat in egg, orange peel and vanilla. Sift together flour, baking powder and salt; gradually add to creamed mixture. Blend in coconut. On lightly floured surface, form into rolls 1½ inches in diameter. Wrap in waxed paper. Chill several hours or overnight. Cut rolls into ⅛-inch slices and place on baking sheets. Bake in 400° oven 5 to 6 minutes. Remove to wire rack to cool. Makes about 11 dozen.

Note: The rolls can be placed in protective wrapping and refrigerated up to 1 week or frozen up to 3 months. If frozen, thaw in refrigerator and bake.

PEANUT BUTTER LEMON ICEBOX COOKIES

2 c. flour	1 c. light brown sugar
1 t. baking soda	
½ t. salt	1 egg
1 c. peanut butter	1 T. grated lemon rind
1 c. butter or margarine	2 T. lemon juice

Sift together flour, soda and salt. Blend together peanut butter and butter. Add sugar gradually, beating until light and fluffy. Beat in egg, lemon rind and juice. Stir in flour mixture, mixing just enough to blend. Shape into two 12-inch rolls—1½ inches in diameter. Wrap in waxed paper. Chill overnight. When ready to bake, cut, using a sawing motion, into ⅛-inch slices. Place on ungreased baking sheet. Bake in 375° oven 8 to 10 minutes. Cool on cookie sheet about 2 minutes before removing to wire rack. Makes 9 dozen cookies.

Pictured opposite
Fabulous Filbert Bars, page 16

COOKIE CONFECTIONS

BUTTERSCOTCH STACKS

1 12-oz. pkg. butterscotch chips
1 1½-oz. can potato sticks
1 c. dry roasted peanuts

Melt butterscotch chips; stir in potato sticks and peanuts. Drop by teaspoons onto waxed paper. Let stand at room temperature until set, about one hour. Makes about 3 dozen.

CHOCOLATE MELTAWAYS

½ c. butter
1 square unsweetened chocolate
¼ c. sugar
1 t. vanilla
1 egg, beaten
2 c. graham cracker crumbs
1 c. flaked coconut
½ c. chopped walnuts

Melt butter and chocolate in saucepan. Blend in sugar, vanilla, egg, crumbs, coconut and nuts. Mix well. Press into a 11½ x 7 x 2-inch pan. Refrigerate until set. Prepare topping and spread over chilled crust.

TOPPING

¼ c. butter
1 T. cream
2 c. confectioners' sugar
1 t. vanilla
1½ squares unsweetened chocolate

Combine butter, cream, sugar and vanilla. Beat until creamy. Spread over crumb mixture. Chill. Melt chocolate and spread evenly over frosting. Chill again. When chocolate is set, but not firm, cut into tiny squares.

COCOA CONFECTIONS

1½ c. vanilla wafer crumbs
½ c. confectioners' sugar
2 T. cocoa
¾ c. finely chopped walnuts
1½ T. corn syrup
3 T. frozen orange juice concentrate
½ t. rum extract
¼ c. finely chopped raisins
Confectioners' sugar
Finely chopped nuts
Cookie crumbs

Combine wafer crumbs with remaining ingredients in large bowl. Shape into 1-inch balls and roll in additional confectioners' sugar, nuts or cookie crumbs. If desired, dip in chocolate coating. Makes about 3 dozen.

FABULOUS FILBERT BARS

1 c. chopped filberts
1 c. butter
1 c. creamy peanut butter
2 6-oz. pkgs. butterscotch chips
5 c. pastel miniature marshmallows
1¾ c. flaked coconut

Toast chopped filberts in 350° oven 5 to 8 minutes. Melt butter, peanut butter, and butterscotch chips together over low heat. Cool slightly. Add marshmallows, filberts and ¾ cup coconut. Mix well. Pat mixture into a buttered 9 x 13-inch pan. Sprinkle on remaining coconut. Cool until firm in refrigerator. Cut into small bars.

GRAHAM SNACKERS

24 graham cracker squares
½ c. butter, melted
½ c. brown sugar
1 c. chopped walnuts

Line an ungreased 15½ x 10½ x 1-inch jelly roll pan with graham cracker squares. Combine butter with brown sugar and spoon over graham crackers. Sprinkle with walnuts. Bake at 350° about 12 minutes. Break into squares. Makes 2 dozen cookies.

NO-BAKE WALNUT BALLS

1 6-oz. pkg. semisweet chocolate chips
1 6-oz. pkg. butterscotch chips
¾ c. confectioners' sugar
½ c. sour cream
1 t. grated orange rind
¼ t. salt
1¾ c. chow mein noodles, crushed
¾ c. ground walnuts

Melt chocolate and butterscotch chips together over hot water in a double boiler; remove from heat. Add rest of ingredients except nuts; mix well. Chill dough 20 minutes. Shape into 1-inch balls; roll in ground walnuts. Store in a tightly covered container. Makes 3½ dozen.

If you don't have time to mix and bake cookies all at once, store the batter in the refrigerator. Bake them later—when it's convenient. Or let the kids do the baking. Cookie batter will keep refrigerated in a tightly covered container for up to a week.

ORANGE CONFECTION BALLS

2¾ c. graham cracker crumbs
1 c. confectioners' sugar, sifted
1 c. finely chopped walnuts
2 T. butter, melted
¼ c. light corn syrup
½ c. frozen orange juice concentrate, thawed
1 3½-oz. can flaked coconut

Combine all ingredients except coconut; mix well. Shape into balls about ¾ inch in diameter. Dip top of each ball into Orange Glaze, then into coconut. Store in air-tight container. Flavor improves with storage. Makes 3½ to 4 dozen.

ORANGE GLAZE

1 c. confectioners' sugar
4 T. frozen orange juice concentrate, thawed

Mix sugar and undiluted orange concentrate together.

CRISPY FRESH ORANGE-GUMDROP COOKIES

1¾ c. flour
½ t. baking soda
¼ t. salt
½ c. shortening
1 c. sugar
1 egg, beaten
1½ T. grated orange peel
⅓ c. fresh orange juice
1 c. gumdrops, cut up
½ c. coarsely chopped walnuts

Sift together flour, soda, and salt. Cream together shortening and sugar until light. Add egg; mix until thoroughly blended. Alternately add sifted dry ingredients and orange juice, beating until smooth. Stir in grated peel, gumdrops and walnuts, blending well. Drop from a teaspoon onto a greased cookie sheet. Bake in a 375° oven, 10 to 12 minutes, or until lightly browned. Remove from oven and let stand about 1 minute before removing to a rack to cool. Cookies will be very crisp. Makes 4 dozen cookies.

CHOCO-PEANUT RING COOKIES

½ c. butter
½ c. sugar
½ c. brown sugar
1 egg
½ t. vanilla
1½ c. flour
½ t. baking soda
½ t. salt
15 small (about 1-inch) peanut butter cup candies, sliced in half crosswise

Beat butter until creamy. Add sugars gradually and beat thoroughly. Beat in egg, then vanilla. Sift together flour, soda and salt; add to creamed mixture. Form into 1¼-inch balls and place on greased cookie sheets; flatten slightly. Press one peanut butter cup candy half in center of each cookie, peanut butter side up. Bake in 375° oven 10 to 12 minutes. Cool on wire racks. Makes 2½ dozen cookies.

COOKIES FROM A MIX

MASTER MIX

9 c. flour
¼ c. baking powder
1 to 1½ T. salt
1½ c. shortening

Stir the baking powder and salt into the flour. Sift three times into a large bowl or pan. Cut in shortening with a pastry blender until the mixture resembles tiny peas or until it is as fine as cornmeal. Store in tightly covered container or in a cool, dry place. Put the mix in a large glass jar or a coffee can lined with a moisture proof plastic bag until baking. Measure into single portions to use. Makes about 13 cups.

BASIC DROP COOKIES

2 c. Master Mix
⅔ c. sugar
1 egg, beaten
1 t. vanilla
½ c. cream (or ⅓ c. milk and 2 T. melted butter)

Stir the sugar into the Master Mix. Combine cream, egg and vanilla. Blend wet and dry ingredients well. Drop by teaspoons onto greased baking sheet. Bake in 375° oven 10 to 12 minutes. Makes 2 to 2½ dozen cookies.

VARIATIONS: Use brown sugar instead of white sugar.

Use 1 tablespoon grated orange or lemon rind in place of vanilla

For chocolate cookies, add 1 square melted chocolate.

Add ½ cup coconut and ½ cup raisins or dates.

Certainly the chocolate chip cookie is an all around winner. This classic American invention first appeared as the original Toll House cookie, named after the famous Toll House Inn at Whitman, Massachusetts. Toll House cookies were introduced to homemakers in 1939 on the radio series Famous Foods from Famous Places.

One story claims this all-American cookie was discovered by accident. One day a home economist used chopped chocolate in her cookie dough instead of raisins. The idea caught on and became popular across the nation. An entirely new industry was created with the invention of the machinery to make the little chocolate pieces.

CHOCOLATE CHIP COOKIES

2 c. Master Mix
½ c. butter or margarine
1 c. brown sugar
1 egg
½ c. chopped nuts
1 6-oz. pkg. semisweet chocolate chips

Mix butter or margarine, sugar and egg together. Stir in rest of ingredients. Drop by teaspoons about 2 inches apart on ungreased baking sheet. Bake in 375° oven 10 minutes or until lightly browned. Makes 4 dozen 1½-inch cookies.

OATMEAL DROP COOKIES

1 c. Master Mix	1 egg, beaten
½ c. sugar	3 T. water
¾ c. uncooked oats	¼ c. raisins
½ t. cinnamon	¼ c. chopped nuts
⅛ t. cloves	

Combine dry ingredients. Add water to beaten egg. Combine liquid with dry ingredients and mix thoroughly. Add raisins and nuts. Stir until well mixed. Drop by teaspoons onto greased baking sheet. Bake in a 400° oven for 10 to 12 minutes, or until browned. Makes 2 dozen medium-sized cookies.

Pictured opposite
Date-Orange Toppers, page 21

TUTTI-FRUTTI COOKIE SQUARES

1 pkg. coconut-pecan snack
  cake mix
2 T. butter, melted
1 T. water
1 t. vinegar
1 8-oz. pkg. cream cheese
1 egg
2 T. sugar
½ c. flaked coconut
¼ c. maraschino cherries, chopped
½ c. crushed pineapple, well drained
¾ c. semisweet chocolate mini-chips

Measure 1½ cups cake mix into a bowl. Stir in butter, water and vinegar; blend well. Pat into greased 9-inch square pan. Bake at 350° about 12 minutes or until firm and lightly browned around edges. Cool about 10 minutes. Thoroughly combine cream cheese, egg and sugar in small bowl. Stir in coconut and cherries; spread over cooled layer in pan. Combine pineapple with remaining cake mix until all cake mix is moistened; add chocolate mini-chips. Crumble onto top of cream cheese layer, covering completely. Bake at 350° for 30 to 35 minutes or until lightly browned. Cool and chill. Cut into 25 squares.

> When you store cookies, make sure soft cookies remain soft; crisp cookies keep crisp. The two types cannot be stored together.

CHEERY CHERRY BARS

1 pkg. spice or apple-spice cake mix
2 eggs
⅓ c. water
6 T. butter, softened
¾ c. dried apricots, chopped
1 3½-oz. can flaked coconut
½ c. maraschino cherries, chopped

In large mixing bowl, beat together cake mix, eggs, water and butter for length of time specified on cake mix. Stir in apricots, coconut and cherries, mixing just until combined. Spread evenly into buttered 15½ x 10½ x 1-inch jelly roll pan. Bake in 375° oven 18 to 20 minutes. Cool in pan on wire rack before cutting. Makes 5 dozen bars.

APPLE RAISIN CRUNCHIES

½ c. butter or margarine
¼ c. milk
1 13¾-oz. pkg. coconut-almond
  frosting mix
2 c. granola
½ c. currants or raisins
½ c. shredded, or finely chopped, apple

In large saucepan, heat butter and milk until butter is melted. Stir in remaining ingredients. Drop by rounded teaspoons 1 inch apart, onto greased cookie sheets. Bake in 325° oven 15 to 20 minutes. Cool 5 minutes before removing. Makes 3 dozen cookies.

CRUNCHY LEMON BARS

1 13¾-oz. pkg. coconut-pecan frosting
  mix
1 c. flour
1 t. baking powder
⅔ c. butter or margarine, softened
1 14-oz. can sweetened condensed milk
1 T. grated lemon peel
½ c. lemon juice

In large mixing bowl, combine dry frosting mix, flour, baking powder and butter; mix until crumbly. Press half of the mixture in an ungreased 8 to 9-inch square baking pan. Combine sweetened condensed milk, lemon peel and juice. Pour over crumb layer. Sprinkle remaining crumbs over filling. Bake in 350° oven for 30 to 40 minutes until golden brown. Cool. Cut into 2 dozen bars.

LEMON COCONUT BARS

½ c. butter
1 lemon cake mix
1 13¾-oz. pkg. lemon fluff frosting mix
1 c. shredded coconut
1 c. chopped walnuts

Cut butter into the dry cake mix. Press and flatten mixture with hand into bottom of ungreased 15½ x 10½-inch pan. Bake at 350° for 5 minutes. Meanwhile, prepare frosting mix as directed on package. Fold in coconut and nutmeats. Spread mixture over baked base. Bake at 350° for 25 minutes or until done. Cool slightly. Cut into bars. Makes 2½ dozen.

EASY BUTTERSCOTCH CRISPIES

½ c. sugar
1 t. baking powder
1 pkg. butterscotch pudding mix
1 c. butter or margarine
1 t. vanilla
2 c. flour
½ c. chopped nuts

In large bowl, combine first five ingredients. Blend thoroughly at medium speed. By hand, stir in flour and nuts. Divide dough into 3 balls. Place each on ungreased cookie sheet. Press into a 9-inch circle; with thumb, press a 1-inch hole in center. Bake in 325° oven 15 to 20 minutes or until edges are lightly browned. Cut each circle into 12 to 16 wedges. Cool 5 minutes. Remove from sheets. Makes about 3 dozen cookies.

Note: Dough may be pressed into a 15 x 10-inch jelly roll pan and cut into squares after baking.

Short of cookie sheets? Try using the aluminum 9 x 13-inch cake pan cover. Or cut pieces of waxed paper the size of your cookie sheets. Place cookie dough on waxed paper. Replace paper with each new batch of cookies.

DATE-ORANGE TOPPERS

1 c. dates, chopped
⅓ c. water
⅓ c. sugar
¼ c. nuts, chopped
1 roll refrigerated slice and bake cookies, any flavor
1 T. orange peel, grated

In saucepan, combine dates, water and sugar. Cook over medium heat, stirring constantly, until mixture thickens. Remove from heat; add nuts. Set aside. Slice cookie dough into 36 slices ¼ inch thick. Place 27 slices on cookie sheets. Place 1 teaspoon of date-nut mixture on top of each slice. Cut remaining 9 slices into thirds. Place each third on top of date-nut mixture. Sprinkle tops with orange peel. Bake in a 350° oven for 10 to 13 minutes or until golden brown. Remove from cookie sheet. Cool. Makes 27 cookies.

CHOCODILES

1 roll refrigerated slice and bake cookies, any flavor
1 6-oz. pkg. milk chocolate or semisweet chocolate chips
1½ c. cornflakes, crushed
½ c. crunchy peanut butter

Slice cookie dough ¼ inch thick and overlap slices in bottom of greased 8- or 9-inch square pan. Bake at 375° for 15 to 20 minutes until lightly brown. (Cookies will be puffy when removed from oven.) Cool slightly. In medium saucepan, melt chocolate pieces. Stir in cornflakes and peanut butter. Spread over cookie base. Cool. Makes 24 bars.

PEPPERMINT REFRESHERS

1 roll refrigerated slice and bake cookies, any flavor
2 egg whites
½ c. sugar
⅛ t. peppermint flavoring
2 T. peppermint stick candy, crushed

Slice cookie dough ¼ inch thick and overlap slices in bottom of greased 8- or 9-inch square pan. Bake at 350° for 15 minutes. (Cookies will be puffy when removed from oven.) Beat egg whites until foamy. Gradually add sugar and continue beating until stiff peaks form. Stir in peppermint flavoring. Spread over baked cookie dough; sprinkle with crushed peppermint candy. Return to oven and bake for 10 minutes. Makes 24 bars.

FRECKLED MALT COOKIES

2 c. flour
1 13¾-oz. pkg. coconut-pecan frosting mix
1 c. malted milk balls, crushed
1 c. butter or margarine, softened
½ t. baking soda
2 eggs, beaten

In large bowl, combine all ingredients; stir until well mixed. Drop by rounded teaspoons, 1 inch apart, onto greased cookie sheets. Bake in 375° oven 8 to 14 minutes or until golden brown. Makes 4 to 5 dozen cookies.

MERINGUE COOKIES

Old-fashioned "kisses" were invented by the thrifty homemaker facing a bowl of leftover egg whites. Today meringue cookies are versatile mouth-watering confections. Tinted or fruit laden, they add an airy festive touch to parties and dinners the year around.

RAISIN KISSES

4 egg whites	2 c. cornflakes
¼ t. salt	1 c. raisins,
1 c. sugar	coarsely chopped
1 t. vanilla	½ c. flaked coconut

Beat egg whites with salt until peaks form. Gradually add sugar, beating until very stiff but not dry. Beat in vanilla. Fold in cornflakes, raisins and coconut. Drop mixture by teaspoons onto lightly greased cookie sheets. Bake in a 350° oven 20 to 25 minutes or until set and golden brown. Immediately remove to racks to cool. Makes about 3 dozen.

APRICOT MERINGUE COOKIES

4 egg whites
⅛ t. salt
1 t. vanilla
1⅓ c. sugar
1 c. dried apricots, diced
½ c. blanched slivered toasted almonds

Beat the egg whites with salt and vanilla in large mixing bowl until soft peaks form. Gradually add the sugar, over a five minute period, beating until a stiff meringue is formed. Fold in the apricots and almonds. Drop by heaping teaspoons onto brown paper-lined or lightly greased baking sheets. Bake in 350° oven for about 20 minutes. Cookies will have a light brown color. Makes about 5 dozen.

COCONUT KISSES

3 egg whites
Dash of salt
1 c. sugar
½ t. vanilla
2 c. cornflakes
1⅓ c. flaked coconut
½ c. chopped pecans
2 1-oz. squares semisweet chocolate
2 t. shortening

Beat egg whites with a dash of salt until foamy; gradually add the sugar, beating to stiff peaks. Stir in vanilla, cornflakes, coconut and pecans. Drop from a teaspoon onto well-greased cookie sheet. Bake at 350° for 18 to 20 minutes. Remove immediately to cooling rack. Melt chocolate with the shortening. Swirl chocolate spiral fashion atop kisses. Makes 3 to 4 dozen kisses. Do not freeze.

Meringue cookies absorb moisture readily. Wrap and store cookies in airtight containers.

PINK KISSES

½ c. superfine granulated sugar
⅛ t. cream of tartar
2 egg whites
Red food coloring
½ c. butter
½ c. confectioners' sugar
1 t. vanilla
1 to 2 T. water

Sift granulated sugar with cream of tartar. Beat egg whites until foamy. Gradually add sugar and continue beating until stiff peaks form. Add food coloring to tint pink. Cover a baking sheet with foil. Using a pastry bag, with star tube, make small swirls of meringue on foil about ½ inch apart. Bake in a 200° oven for 1 hour or until dry. Cool and remove from baking sheet; store in a tightly covered container. About 1 hour before serving, cream butter, confectioners' sugar and vanilla, adding enough water to reach spreading consistency. Spread bottom of each meringue kiss with frosting and put together in pairs. Refrigerate until serving time. Makes about 4 dozen.

Pictured opposite
Apricot Unbeatables, page 25

FLAVORFUL FRUIT COOKIES

RAISIN LEMON TOFFEE COOKIES

½ c. butter, softened
1½ c. sugar
1 egg
1 egg yolk
1½ t. lemon juice
1 T. grated lemon peel
2¼ c. flour
1½ t. baking powder
½ t. salt
½ c. milk
¾ c. raisins
Toffee Topping

Cream butter and sugar until fluffy. Stir in egg, egg yolk, lemon juice and lemon peel. Beat until well blended. Sift together flour, baking powder and salt. Add flour mixture to creamed mixture alternately with milk. Stir in raisins. Drop from teaspoon onto lightly greased cookie sheet, allowing room for spreading. Bake in 350° oven 10 to 15 minutes, or until cookies are lightly golden. Frost each cookie with thin layer of Toffee Topping. Place under broiler and broil until bubbly. Allow to cool. Makes about 3½ dozen cookies.

TOFFEE TOPPING

½ c. slivered almonds
6 T. butter
⅔ c. brown sugar
2 T. flour
2 T. milk

Spread almonds evenly on a cookie sheet; bake at 350° for 5 minutes or until toasted. Combine almonds with remaining ingredients in a saucepan and stir over medium-low heat until bubbly.

BEST RAISIN OATMEAL COOKIES

⅔ c. shortening, melted
1 c. brown sugar
1 egg
1 t. vanilla
1 c. flour
1 t. salt
1 t. baking powder
2 c. uncooked oats
1 c. raisins

Beat together shortening, brown sugar, egg and vanilla. Sift together dry ingredients; add to shortening mixture; beat well. Stir in oats and raisins. Drop by teaspoons onto greased cookie sheets. Bake at 350° 15 to 20 minutes. Remove to racks to cool. Makes about 5 dozen cookies.

Mankind has been preserving fruits by drying since the beginning of recorded history. He certainly discovered grapes drying on the vines thousands of years ago.

The word raisin comes from the Latin "racemus" which means a cluster of grapes or berries; and a raisin is a dried grape.

The dried fruit industry in this nation is indebted to the Mission Fathers who established the chain of California missions. The friars planted the first peaches, apricots, black Mission figs and raisin grapes.

It looked like a tragedy to California grape growers when their grapes dried on the vines during the long, hot summer of 1873. In desperation, one grower shipped his crop to market anyway; and California's first commercial raisins sold like the proverbial hot cakes. Their popularity has never waned.

SPICY RAISIN BARS

1 c. sifted flour
½ t. baking soda
½ t. salt
1 t. pumpkin pie spice
½ c. shortening
½ c. brown sugar
¼ c. milk
1 t. vanilla
1 c. uncooked oats
1 c. raisins

Sift together flour, soda, salt and spice. Add shortening, sugar, milk and vanilla. Beat until smooth (about 2 minutes). Blend in oats and raisins. Spread batter evenly in greased 11 x 7-inch baking pan. Bake in 350° oven 20 to 25 minutes. Cut into bars. Makes 2 dozen spicy raisin bars.

RAISIN CRISSCROSS COOKIES

½ c. butter	¾ t. cream of
¾ c. sugar	tartar
1 egg	¾ t. baking soda
½ t. lemon extract	½ t. salt
1¾ c. flour	1 c. raisins

Combine butter, sugar, egg, and lemon flavoring. Mix well. Sift together flour, cream of tartar, soda, and salt. Stir into butter mixture. Mix in raisins. Roll in 1-inch balls. Place about 3 inches apart on ungreased baking sheet. Flatten with fork dipped in flour, making a crisscross pattern. Bake 8 to 10 minutes in a 400° oven. Cool on rack. Makes about 3 dozen cookies.

APRICOT UNBEATABLES

2 c. confectioners' sugar
½ c. flour
½ t. baking powder
½ c. (3 to 4) egg whites
2 c. chopped walnuts
½ c. dried apricots, chopped

Combine sugar, flour, baking powder and egg whites. Add walnuts and apricots; mix well. Drop by teaspoons onto well-greased cookie sheets. Bake at 325° for 15 to 18 minutes. Cool on rack. Makes 3 dozen cookies.

A is for apples, B is for best and C, of course, is for cookie. Apples, either freshly chopped or in a sauce, lend a lovely moist texture to cookies.

Every school child knows the legend of Johnny Appleseed and how he spread apple seeds and graftings of trees across the nation. Apples, one of nature's most perfect health foods, flourished and are now grown commercially in thirty-five states. The first patent on canned apple cider was issued in 1862. Seven years later, in 1869, canned applesauce received a patent. However, it wasn't until 1920 that quantities of apples and applesauce were canned commercially.

FROSTY APPLESAUCE COOKIES

1 c. butter	½ t. salt
1 c. brown sugar	½ t. baking powder
1 egg	½ t. allspice
1 8½-oz. can	¼ t. cloves
applesauce	1 c. whole bran
1 T. molasses	cereal
2 c. flour	1 c. raisins

Cream butter and brown sugar. Blend in egg, applesauce and molasses. Sift together flour, salt, baking powder and spices and stir into batter. Fold in cereal and raisins. Drop by teaspoons onto ungreased cookie sheet. Bake at 350° for 15 minutes. Cool and frost with Caramel Frosting. Makes 5 dozen cookies.

CARAMEL FROSTING

½ c. brown sugar
¼ c. butter or margarine, melted
3½ T. milk
1½ c. confectioners' sugar, sifted

Add brown sugar to butter; boil and stir for 1 minute. Cool slightly. Beat in milk. Add confectioners' sugar and beat until smooth.

SPICED APPLESAUCE COOKIES

½ c. shortening
1 c. sugar
1 egg
2 c. flour
1 t. salt
1 t. baking soda
1 t. baking powder
¼ t. cloves
1 t. cinnamon
1 c. thick, unsweetened applesauce

Cream shortening. Add sugar gradually, creaming until light. Beat in egg. Sift dry ingredients together and add alternately with the applesauce. Blend thoroughly. Drop by teaspoons on greased cookie sheet about 2 inches apart. Bake in 350° oven 10 minutes or until nicely browned. Remove from pan to cool. Makes about 3 dozen cookies.

APPLE TEA STICKS

¾ c. flour
1 t. baking powder
½ t. cinnamon
¼ t. salt
1 egg
¾ c. light brown sugar
¼ c. milk
1 t. vanilla
½ c. peanut butter
1 c. raw apples, chopped

Sift flour with baking powder, cinnamon and salt. Beat egg until light and gradually beat in sugar. Stir in milk, vanilla and peanut butter. Fold in flour mixture and apples. Spread in greased square pan 8 x 8 x 2 inches. Bake in 350° oven 30 to 35 minutes. Cool in pan for about 5 minutes. Cut into 24 finger-shaped pieces. Roll in sifted confectioners' sugar. Makes 24 sticks.

MOIST CRANBERRY-APPLE COOKIES

½ c. butter or margarine
1 c. brown sugar
¾ c. sugar
1 egg
¼ c. milk
2 c. flour
1 t. baking powder
1 t. cinnamon
½ t. salt
1 t. grated orange rind
1½ c. pared apples, chopped
1 c. cranberries, chopped

Cream butter and sugars; beat in egg and milk. Sift together flour, baking powder, cinnamon and salt. Stir into butter mixture until well blended. Stir in orange rind, apple and cranberries. Drop by teaspoons onto greased cookie sheets. Bake at 375° for 12 to 15 minutes. Makes about 4 dozen cookies.

When you are using an old-time recipe that calls for brown sugar, you may not need to pack down the sugar. Modern recipes, however, require that brown sugar be packed down in measuring.

CHERRY CHOCOLATE CHIP COOKIES

1¼ c. flour
½ t. salt
½ t. baking soda
½ c. butter or margarine
½ c. sugar
¼ c. dark brown sugar
1 egg
½ c. red maraschino cherries, drained and chopped
¼ c. chopped walnuts
1 6-oz. pkg. semisweet chocolate chips

Sift together flour, salt and baking soda. Cream butter with sugars; beat in egg. Stir in cherries, walnuts, chocolate pieces and sifted dry ingredients. Drop rounded teaspoons of batter on ungreased baking sheets, about 1 inch apart. Bake in 375° oven 8 to 10 minutes. Let stand ½ minute, then remove from baking sheets. Makes about 4 dozen.

BANANA TURNOVER COOKIES

1⅓ c. flour
¼ t. salt
¼ t. cinnamon
¼ c. oil
½ c. creamed cottage cheese
1½ T. honey
2 bananas, sliced
¼ c. raisins
2 T. sunflower seeds

Mix together flour, salt and cinnamon. Add oil and stir until mixture resembles coarse meal. Mix together cottage cheese and honey; stir into flour mixture and form into a ball. Roll out ¼ of dough at a time on a board (it is not necessary to sprinkle flour over the board); cut into 4-inch rounds. Place 3 banana slices on half of each dough round. Add 1 teaspoon raisins and ½ teaspoon sunflower seeds to banana slices. Fold far end of dough over filling, to form a turnover. Seal edges. Place on ungreased baking sheet. Bake in 400° oven 10 minutes. Remove and cool. Sprinkle top with confectioners' sugar before serving. Makes 12 turnovers.

NECTARINE COUNTRY COOKIES

1½ c. nectarines, chopped
2 c. flour
1 t. baking soda
1 t. salt
¼ t. cinnamon
⅛ t. cloves
½ c. butter
1⅓ c. sugar
1 egg
½ c. diced roasted almonds
½ c. raisins

Sift flour with soda, salt, cinnamon and cloves. Cream butter with sugar; mix in egg, almonds and raisins. Alternately add flour mixture and chopped nectarines. Drop by tablespoons onto greased baking sheet. Bake at 375° for 13 to 15 minutes. Cool on rack. Store in loosely covered container. Makes 3 to 4 dozen cookies.

Follow the recipe carefully in cooling the cookies—in the pan or on a wire rack. Do not stack, pile or overlap warm cookies. Allow them to cool completely before storing.

CHOCOLATE-APRICOT COOKIES

¼ c. butter or margarine
¼ c. shortening
⅓ c. light brown sugar
⅓ c. sugar
1 egg
½ t. vanilla
1 c. flour
½ t. salt
½ t. baking soda
⅔ c. dried apricots, finely chopped
½ c. semisweet chocolate chips or chopped nuts

Cream together butter, shortening and sugars. Beat in egg and vanilla. Sift together flour, salt and soda; stir into creamed mixture until smooth. Stir in apricots and chocolate pieces. Drop by rounded half-teaspoons onto ungreased baking sheets. Bake in 375° oven 8 to 10 minutes or until lightly browned. Cool on wire racks. Makes about 4 dozen 2-inch cookies.

LEMON LASSIES

2¼ c. flour
1 t. cinnamon
½ t. baking soda
¼ t. salt
½ c. butter or margarine
1 c. sugar
1 egg
¼ c. light molasses

Sift flour with cinnamon, soda and salt. Cream margarine and sugar. Add egg and molasses. Add dry ingredients gradually. Mix well. Divide dough in half. Press half of dough over bottom of an ungreased 13 x 9-inch glass baking dish. Spread with cooled Filling. Chill. Chill remaining half of dough at least 2 hours; then roll out to ⅛-inch thickness between 2 pieces of waxed paper. Place on top of Filling. Bake at 325° for 30 minutes. When slightly cool, cut into bars and remove from dish.

FILLING

2 eggs, slightly beaten
½ c. sugar
1 T. grated lemon peel
¼ c. lemon juice
1 T. butter or margarine
⅛ t. salt
1 c. grated coconut

In pan, combine eggs, sugar, lemon peel, lemon juice, margarine and salt. Cook over low heat, stirring constantly until thick. Remove from heat. Add coconut. Cool.

Sparkling tart red cranberries add an eye-pleasing note to homemade cookies.

Long before the signing of the Declaration of Independence, cranberries grew wild in the United States. The Indians used the berry as a fruit, a dye and as a first-aid remedy.

Though cranberries have always been a part of Thanksgiving, you need not only prepare them in traditional ways. They combine well with other fruits and make a perfect moist cookie.

FRESH ORANGE-CRANBERRY COOKIES

2¼ c. flour
½ t. baking soda
½ t. salt
½ c. butter, softened
½ c. sugar
½ c. brown sugar
1 egg
½ t. vanilla
½ c. orange, unpeeled but finely chopped
¾ c. whole cranberry sauce, drained
1 c. coarsely chopped walnuts

Sift together flour, soda and salt. Cream the butter and sugars until fluffy. Add egg and vanilla. Blend well. To butter mixture alternately add dry ingredients and chopped orange and cranberry sauce. Blend thoroughly. Stir in nutmeats. Drop by teaspoons onto lightly greased cookie sheets. Bake at 375° for 10 to 12 minutes. Cookies will be crisp when cool. Makes 4 dozen cookies.

MIXED-UP FRUITCAKE COOKIES

½ c. butter or margarine
1 c. sugar
1 egg
¼ c. water
¼ t. brandy extract
1½ c. flour
1¼ t. baking powder
¼ t. salt
1 t. cinnamon
¼ t. nutmeg
¼ t. allspice
½ c. dried apricots, chopped
½ c. raisins
¼ c. mixed candied fruits
½ c. chopped walnuts

Cream butter and sugar until light. Beat in egg, water and brandy extract. Sift together flour, baking powder, salt and spices; gradually stir into butter mixture. Add fruits and nuts. Mix thoroughly. Drop from teaspoons onto ungreased baking sheet. Bake in 400° oven 8 minutes or until lightly browned. Cool on rack. Makes 3 dozen cookies.

LEMON BLENDER COOKIES

1 lemon
6 T. water
½ c. shortening
1 egg
1 pkg. yellow cake mix

Trim a thin slice from both ends of unpeeled lemon; cut in half lengthwise. Make a shallow V-shape cut; remove white center core. Cut halves in small chunks. In electric blender, puree lemon chunks, adding water. Add shortening and egg; blend until smooth. In large bowl, combine cake mix and lemon mixture; mix well. Drop batter from teaspoons on lightly greased cookie sheets. Bake at 350° for 13 to 15 minutes. Cool on wire racks. Makes about 5 dozen cookies.

CHERRY OATMEAL COOKIES

½ c. shortening
½ c. butter
1 c. dark brown sugar
1 c. sugar
2 eggs
1 t. vanilla
1½ c. flour
1 t. baking powder
½ t. baking soda
½ t. salt
1 c. red maraschino cherries, drained and chopped
½ c. flaked coconut
2 c. uncooked oats
Red maraschino cherries, drained and cut in pieces for decoration

Cream together shortening, butter, and sugars until light and fluffy. Beat in eggs and vanilla. Sift together flour, baking powder, soda and salt. Gradually add 1 cup chopped cherries, coconut, oats and sifted dry ingredients to creamed mixture. Chill 1 hour. Drop rounded tablespoons of batter on ungreased baking sheets. Place a piece of maraschino cherry (well-drained) atop each cookie. Bake in 375° oven 10 to 12 minutes or until golden brown. After 1 minute, remove cookies to racks and cool. Makes about 6 dozen cookies.

Peanut Brittle Cookies

Uncle Gerry & Aunt Diane ✓
Charlie & Kathy ✓
Aunt Carol ✓
Owens Family ✓
Darlene K.
Pastor Pingry
Grandma & Grandpa Haslam

Dr. Callahan

Get more tins !!

NUT FLAVORED COOKIES

Generally the cookie jar is either half full or half empty. It all depends on who you ask, the cookie baker or the cookie eater. However, both will agree that sweet, moist coconut is a succulent addition to a favorite cookie.

Coconut was known as the Indian nut during Biblical times. During the sixteenth century some called it Nargil. This name was dropped by the eighteenth century and cocoanut became the new name. Forty years later, we Americanized the name to coconut.

Coconut, mainly known for its snowy whiteness, is available to cookie bakers in flaked, shredded or grated form. Each form provides a unique texture to enhance your favorite cookie.

COCO-CHOCO-NUT COOKIES

2¼ c. flour
1 t. baking soda
1 t. salt
1 c. margarine or butter
¾ c. sugar
¾ c. brown sugar
1 t. vanilla
½ t. water
2 eggs
1 c. flaked or shredded coconut
1 c. coarsely chopped nuts
1 6-oz. pkg. semisweet chocolate chips

Sift flour, soda and salt together. Blend butter, sugars, vanilla and water until smooth. Beat in eggs. Add flour mixture gradually, stirring well. Fold in coconut, nuts and chocolate chips. Drop by teaspoons onto greased cookie sheet. Bake at 350° for 10 minutes or until lightly browned. Makes about 9 dozen cookies.

COCONUT CHERRY BARS

1 c. margarine or butter
1¼ c. sugar
1 egg
1 t. vanilla
2½ c. flour
1½ t. baking powder
½ t. salt
½ c. chopped nuts
½ c. maraschino cherries, chopped
⅔ c. flaked coconut
1 6-oz. pkg. chocolate chips

Cream margarine or butter; add sugar gradually. Blend in egg and vanilla. Sift together flour, baking powder and salt. Stir into creamed mixture. Add nuts, cherries, coconut and chocolate chips. Spread dough in a greased 13 x 9-inch pan. Bake at 375° for about 25 minutes or until bars are firm in the center. Cool slightly; cut into 40 bars.

Note: These delightful bars, popular all year around, are an attractive addition to your Christmas cookie tray. Bake a second batch using green maraschino cherries instead of red cherries. Or use ¼ cup each red or green maraschino cherries for a festive holiday touch.

COCONUT PEANUT BUTTER CRISPS

2 c. flour
1½ t. baking powder
¼ t. salt
½ c. butter
½ c. peanut butter
1 c. brown sugar
1 egg
2 T. honey
1 c. flaked coconut

Sift flour with baking powder and salt. Cream butter, peanut butter and sugar together until light and fluffy. Beat in egg and honey. Fold in flour mixture until blended. Stir in coconut. Shape into rolls about 2 inches in diameter. Wrap in waxed paper and chill in refrigerator overnight or until firm. Slice ⅛ inch thick. Bake on an ungreased baking sheet in a 375° oven for about 12 minutes. Makes about 6 dozen cookies.

PEANUT BRITTLE COOKIES

1 c. flour	1 egg
¼ t. baking soda	1 t. vanilla
½ t. cinnamon	1 c. finely chopped
½ c. butter	salted peanuts
½ c. brown sugar	

Sift together flour, soda and cinnamon. Gradually add brown sugar to butter. Cream well. Blend in two tablespoons beaten egg (reserve remaining egg) and 1 teaspoon vanilla. Add dry ingredients and ½ cup peanuts. Mix thoroughly. Spread or pat dough on 15 x 10 x 2-inch greased baking sheet. Brush with remaining egg. Sprinkle with remaining peanuts. Bake in a 325° oven 20 to 25 minutes. Do not overbake. Cut or break into pieces while warm.

Crispy, crunchy, delicious cookies filled with peanuts are especially good.

Peanuts were grown thousands of years ago in South America. Peanut-shaped pottery and peanut designs have been found in Inca tombs. Spanish explorers discovered peanuts in Peru. They took them to Spain and traded them to Africans. In time, African slaves brought them to America.

The peanut fame in the United States is credited to the Civil War, the Circus and baseball.

SALTED PEANUT COOKIES

1 c. butter or margarine
1 c. granulated sugar
1 c. dark brown sugar
2 eggs
1 t. vanilla
1½ c. flour
1 t. baking soda
3 c. uncooked oats
1½ c. salted peanuts

Cream butter and sugars. Add unbeaten eggs and vanilla, beating until fluffy. Sift flour with soda; add oats. Stir in dry ingredients. Add peanuts, mixing well. Drop by rounded teaspoons onto ungreased cookie sheet. Bake at 375° for 12 minutes. Makes 6 dozen.

PEANUT CHOCOLATE CHIP COOKIES

¼ c. butter or margarine
¼ c. shortening
2 T. peanut butter
½ c. sugar
½ c. light brown sugar
1 egg
1 t. vanilla
1¾ c. flour
½ t. baking soda
½ t. salt
1 c. salted Spanish peanuts
1 6-oz. pkg. semisweet chocolate chips

Cream butter, shortening and peanut butter until soft and fluffy. Stir in sugars, egg and vanilla. Add dry ingredients. Fold in peanuts and chocolate chips. Drop by teaspoons on ungreased cookie sheets about 2 inches apart. Bake in 375° oven 8 to 10 minutes, or until edges of cookies are lightly browned. Cool cookies 5 minutes on cookie sheet. Remove and cool on a rack. Makes 4 dozen.

CRUNCHY PEANUT COOKIES

½ c. butter	3 t. baking powder
½ c. peanut butter	½ t. salt
¾ c. sugar	1 c. raisins
2 eggs	1 c. salted peanuts
½ c. milk	3 c. cornflakes
2 c. flour	

Cream butter and peanut butter. Stir in sugar, eggs and milk. Sift together flour, baking powder and salt. Add to creamed mixture, beating until smooth. Fold in raisins, peanuts and cornflakes. Drop by heaping teaspoons on greased cookie sheets. Bake in a 350° oven for 15 minutes or until lightly browned. Cool cookies on a rack. Store in tightly covered container in a cool dry place. Makes about 60 2-inch cookies.

Always cover any butter cookie dough while in the refrigerator. This will prevent the delicate dough from absorbing other food flavors and drying out.

WALNUT SCOTCHIES

1 6-oz. pkg. butterscotch chips
¾ c. butter
2 T. boiling water
1 t. baking soda
1½ c. uncooked oats
1 c. flour
1 c. chopped walnuts
¾ c. sugar
¼ t. salt

Melt butterscotch chips and butter. Remove from heat. Add the boiling water with baking soda and mix well. Gradually blend in remaining ingredients. Drop by slightly rounded teaspoons, 2 inches apart on ungreased baking sheets. Bake at 350° for 10 minutes. Makes 5 dozen.

GERMAN WALNUT CAKES

1¼ c. flour
⅓ c. sugar
½ c. butter
2 T. milk
½ t. vanilla
½ c. chopped walnuts
1 to 1½ c. walnuts, halves and
    large pieces
    Glaze
4 oz. semisweet or milk chocolate

Combine flour and sugar. Cut in butter until particles are very fine. Sprinkle milk and vanilla over mixture and mix to a stiff dough. Mix in chopped walnuts. Roll dough ¼-inch thick on lightly floured board and cut into rounds. Place on ungreased baking sheet. Cover each cookie with walnut half or piece, pressing them lightly into dough. Bake at 350° for 15 minutes, until edges are very lightly browned. Remove to wire rack and set on baking sheet. Drizzle tops with hot Glaze. Cool. Melt chocolate over warm (not hot) water. Spread bottom of each cookie with chocolate and place on waxed paper until chocolate is set. Makes 2 dozen 2-inch cookies.

GLAZE

⅓ c. dark brown sugar
⅓ c. light corn syrup

Combine sugar and syrup in small saucepan; stir over moderate heat until sugar is dissolved. Boil one minute.

Butter can be taken directly from the refrigerator and creamed if you cut each stick into about eight pieces. Keep the mixer speed low when starting the creaming. This method is better than allowing the butter to soften before using. If butter becomes too soft, it means adding extra flour to the dough and that cuts down on the shortness or tenderness of the cookies.

DOUBLE SWIRL WALNUT COOKIES

¾ c. shortening (half butter)
1¼ c. sugar
2 eggs
1 t. vanilla
2½ c. flour
1 t. baking powder
1 t. salt
2 squares unsweetened chocolate
2 T. milk
⅔ c. finely chopped walnuts

Beat together shortening, sugar, eggs and vanilla until fluffy. Sift flour with baking powder and salt. Blend into creamed mixture. Divide dough in half. Blend melted chocolate, milk and half the walnuts into one portion; blend remaining walnuts into light dough. Wrap each portion in waxed paper; chill thoroughly. Roll light dough on lightly floured board to a 8 x 12-inch rectangle. Cover with a sheet of waxed paper and top with a baking sheet. Invert all, remove board and refrigerate dough while rolling chocolate portion to same size. Place light dough over chocolate dough, with shorter sides matching and one longer side about ¼ inch in from edge of chocolate portion. Cut crosswise through center, making two 6-inch sections for easier rolling. Starting from side showing chocolate dough, roll the two together to center. Turn over and roll from the other side to meet the first roll. Wrap in waxed paper and chill until very firm. Cut rolls into ¼-inch slices and place on lightly greased baking sheets. Bake at 400° for about 8 minutes. Let stand a minute, then remove carefully with broad spatula and cool on wire racks. Makes about 40 cookies.

Anytime is a grand time for sampling oven-fresh cookies. A fine addition to any cookie recipe is crisp, crunchy walnuts. The mellow flavor combines well with lively spices. Walnuts are the number one cookie nut.

Walnuts are international travelers. In Biblical times they were grown and eaten in ancient Persia. Traded and transplanted, walnuts eventually reached Italy, Spain and France. English ships carried walnuts all over the world. In time, they became incorrectly known as "English" walnuts. However, they were never commercially grown in England.

In the 1700s Spanish missionaries brought walnuts to California. The trees thrived in the warm climate and rich soil. California now claims to be the walnut capital of the world.

WALNUT PINWHEELS

⅔ c. butter
1 c. sugar
1 egg
1 t. vanilla
1 t. grated lemon peel
2 T. milk
2½ c. flour
½ t. salt
½ t. baking powder
¾ c. finely chopped walnuts
⅓ c. brown sugar
¼ c. honey
12 candied cherries, halved

Cream butter and sugar. Add egg, vanilla, lemon peel and milk. Sift flour with salt and baking powder; blend into creamed mixture to make stiff dough. Chill about 1 hour. Combine walnuts, brown sugar and honey and mix well for filling. Roll half of chilled dough on lightly floured board to 9 x 12-inch rectangle and cut into 3-inch squares. Place teaspoonful of filling in center of each. Cut diagonally from corners of squares toward center, making 8 points. Fold every other point to center over filling. Press cherry half in center of each. Lift with a broad spatula onto lightly greased baking sheet. Bake at 350° about 12 to 14 minutes. Makes 2 dozen cookies.

WALNUT JAM CRESCENTS

1⅓ c. flour
¼ t. salt
⅔ c. butter or margarine
½ c. sour cream
⅔ c. walnuts
⅔ c. raspberry jam or orange marmalade

Combine flour with salt. Cut in butter until in fine particles. Add sour cream and mix to a stiff dough. Divide into two even-size portions. Shape each into a round. Wrap in waxed paper and chill well. Meanwhile, chop walnuts very fine. Roll one portion of chilled pastry at a time to an 11-inch round on lightly floured board. Spread with ⅓ cup jam and sprinkle with ⅓ cup walnuts. Cut into quarters, then cut each quarter into 3 wedges. Roll up, one at a time, starting from outer edge, and place on lightly greased cookie sheet. Repeat with second pastry round. Bake in upper half of oven at 375° for 25 to 30 minutes, until lightly browned. Remove to wire racks to cool. Makes 2 dozen crescents.

WALNUT DIAGONALS

¾ c. butter
½ c. sugar
¼ t. salt
2 egg yolks
1 t. vanilla
2 c. flour
1 c. walnuts, chopped
½ c. brown sugar
¼ c. sour cream
Dash nutmeg

Cream together butter, sugar and salt. Beat in egg yolks and vanilla. Blend in flour. Chill dough about ½ hour. Roll half the cookie dough to a rectangle about 6 x 15-inches. Cut lengthwise into three 2 x 15-inch strips and transfer carefully to cookie sheet, using wide spatula. Put remaining dough through a cookie press fitted with star plate. Force dough along sides and ends of dough strips. (If cookie press is not available, shape dough into ropes about the diameter of a pencil and place along sides and ends of dough strips.) Mix walnuts with brown sugar, sour cream and nutmeg. Spoon this walnut mixture in center and along length of dough. Bake at 350° for 20 to 25 minutes or until lightly browned. Cool, then cut into diagonal slices. Makes about 3 dozen cookies.

Pictured opposite
Double Swirl Walnut Cookies, page 33

The almond is a delicious nut, found in many cookie recipes around the world.

Blanched, unblanched, grated, ground, slivered, chopped and sliced, almonds are the aristocrats of the cookie nuts.

ALMOND SNOWBALL COOKIES

2 c. cornflakes
1 c. butter or margarine
½ c. sugar
1 egg
2 t. vanilla
1¾ c. flour
½ t. salt
2 c. finely chopped almonds
1½ c. confectioners' sugar

Crush cornflakes into fine crumbs. Set aside. Cream butter and sugar until light and fluffy. Add egg and vanilla and beat well. Sift together flour and salt. With pastry blender, cut flour mixture into butter mixture. Stir in crumbs and almonds. Shape level tablespoons of dough into balls and place on ungreased baking sheets. Bake in 350° oven about 20 minutes or until lightly browned. Cool slightly on baking sheets. Roll in confectioners'sugar. Cool completely before serving. Makes about 5 dozen 1-inch balls.

COCONUT ALMOND COOKIES

1 c. butter
¼ t. salt
1 c. confectioners' sugar
1 t. almond extract
1 c. finely grated coconut
2¼ c. cake flour
¾ c. ground blanched almonds
Confectioners' sugar

Cream butter with salt. Gradually add sugar, creaming until light and fluffy. Blend in almond extract and coconut. Add flour a little at a time. Stir in almonds. Chill dough. Form into crescents; place on ungreased baking sheets. Bake in 325° oven 18 to 20 minutes. Cool on sheets. Sprinkle with confectioners' sugar. Makes about 4½ dozen cookies.

Roll one *uncut* roll of refrigerated cookie dough in chopped nuts, slice and bake. Or slice refrigerated cookie dough, press each slice into finely chopped nuts to coat both sides and bake.

BROWN SUGAR ALMOND COOKIES

¾ c. butter
2 c. brown sugar
2 eggs
1 t. vanilla
3 c. flour
2 t. baking powder
¾ t. salt
1 c. finely chopped almonds
Whole almonds
Red or green candied cherries
Clear Glaze

Thoroughly mix butter, sugar, eggs and vanilla. Blend in flour, baking powder and salt. Stir in almonds. On lightly floured surface roll dough ⅛ inch thick. Cut into circles. Place on ungreased baking sheet. Decorate with whole almonds and cherries. Bake in 375° oven 5 to 7 minutes or until very lightly browned. Brush cooled cookies with Clear Glaze. Makes about 5 dozen 3-inch cookies.

CLEAR GLAZE

Heat ¼ cup light corn syrup and 2 tablespoons water just to a rolling boil. Cool to lukewarm.

While the pecans' major claim to fame is in pie, do not overlook this nut in cookie baking. It is second only to the walnut in versatility.

The pecan tree grows tall, sometimes reaching over 180 feet. The tree is native to Mississippi and Alabama. Depending on where you look, you'll hear them called pecawns, peecans, Illinois nuts, Mississippi nuts or Natchez nuts.

Indians used pecans in every possible way, including ground in stews and mixed with beans.

COCOA PECAN PUFFS

1 c. butter
1½ c. brown sugar
1 egg
1 18¼-oz. can crushed pineapple
3½ c. flour
3 T. cocoa
1 t. baking powder
1 t. cinnamon
½ t. salt
½ c. chopped pecans

Cream butter and sugar until fluffy. Beat in egg until well blended. Fold in pineapple with the syrup. Combine flour, cocoa, baking powder, cinnamon and salt. Stir into pineapple mixture. Fold in pecans. Drop by teaspoons onto lightly greased baking sheets. Bake in 375° oven 12 to 15 minutes or until lightly browned around edges. Remove to racks to cool before storing. Makes 4 to 4½ dozen cookies.

MILK CHOCOLATE PECAN BARS

1 c. flour   ¼ c. butter
½ c. brown sugar   Topping
½ t. baking soda   ½ c. pecans
¼ t. salt

In large bowl, combine flour, brown sugar, baking soda and salt; mix well. Cut in butter with pastry blender until mixture resembles fine crumbs. Press evenly into a greased 13 x 9 x 2-inch baking pan. Bake at 350° for 10 minutes. Pour Topping over cookie base; sprinkle with pecans. Return to oven and bake at 350° for 20 minutes. Cool; cut into 4 dozen 2 x 1-inch bars.

TOPPING

2 c. milk chocolate chips
2 eggs
¼ c. brown sugar
1 t. vanilla
1 t. salt
½ c. chopped pecans

Melt milk chocolate morsels over hot (not boiling) water; remove from heat. In small bowl, combine eggs, brown sugar, vanilla and salt. Beat 2 minutes at high speed on electric mixer. Add melted chocolate; mix well. Stir in pecans.

LEMON FROSTED PECAN COOKIES

1 c. butter or margarine
¾ c. confectioners' sugar
2 T. milk
1½ c. flour
¾ c. cornstarch
¾ c. chopped pecans
2½ c. confectioners' sugar
1 T. butter
3 T. lemon juice
Yellow food coloring

Stir butter to soften. Add confectioners' sugar, milk, flour and cornstarch. Cream until well blended; chill. Place small spoonfuls of chopped pecans 2 inches apart on an ungreased baking sheet. Shape dough into small balls (about 1 teaspoon) and flatten each over a few pecans. Bake in 350° oven for 12 to 15 minutes. Cool. Combine remaining ingredients. Spread over cookies. Makes 4 dozen.

GIFTS OF LOVE

It's time to make another batch
Of cookies good and sweet
To keep the jar brimming full
Of fresh-baked cookie treats.

There's nothing quite as pleasing
When a friend drops in for tea,
As delicious homemade cookies
That demand the recipe!

And when the children return from school,
As hungry as can be,
Fill them up with milk and cookies
And special memories.

So keep the jar upon the shelf
Brimming full indeed
Of confections you have made,
Gifts of love are these!

Betty Dollar Wallace

OLD-FASHIONED CEREAL AND GRAIN COOKIES

CANDIED OATMEAL DROPS

1 c. candied citron or glazed cherries, halves
¼ c. brandy
1½ c. flour
1 t. salt
1 t. cinnamon
½ t. baking soda
½ t. cloves
1 c. brown sugar
¾ c. butter or shortening
2 eggs, beaten
3 c. uncooked oats
1 c. chopped nuts

Soak candied fruit in brandy while preparing dough, or soak overnight. Stir together flour, salt, cinnamon, soda and cloves. Beat together sugar, butter and eggs. Stir in flour mixture, then fold in soaked fruit, oats and nuts. Drop by level tablespoons onto lightly greased baking sheets. Bake in 375° oven 10 to 12 minutes or until lightly brown. Cool. Makes 5½ dozen.

There are cookies and there are cookies, but oatmeal cookies are always special. These welcome and nourishing cookies have kept cookie jars filled for generations.

Perhaps the forerunner of our classic oatmeal cookie is the Scottish oatcake or bannock. The oatcakes are made in circles, then cut in wedges called farls.

Oats arrived in the Colonies in the early 1600s. Creative early American cooks gradually incorporated oats into a vast array of recipes. Most of us will agree the oatmeal cookie was the best invention of all.

CHEWY OATMEAL COOKIES

1 c. flour
1 t. cinnamon
¾ t. baking soda
½ t. salt
¼ t. nutmeg
¾ c. shortening
1⅓ c. brown sugar
2 eggs
1 t. vanilla
2 c. uncooked oats
1 c. raisins

Sift together flour, cinnamon, soda, salt and nutmeg. Cream shortening and sugar. Add eggs and vanilla; beat until smooth. Add flour mixture. Stir in oatmeal and raisins. Drop rounded teaspoons of dough onto greased cookie sheets. Bake in 350° oven 12 to 15 minutes. Makes about 3½ dozen cookies.

CEREAL 'N CHOCOLATE CHIP COOKIES

1¾ c. flour
1 t. baking soda
½ t. salt
1 c. butter or margarine
¾ c. granulated sugar
¾ c. brown sugar
2 eggs
1 t. vanilla
2 c. oven-toasted rice cereal
1 6-oz. pkg. semisweet chocolate chips

Stir together flour, soda and salt. Set aside. Cream together butter and sugars. Add egg and vanilla and beat well. Stir in dry ingredients. Add rice cereal and chocolate chips. Drop by level tablespoons onto greased baking sheets. Bake in 350° oven about 10 minutes or until lightly browned. Cool about 1 minute before removing from baking sheets. Place on wire racks. Makes about 6 dozen 2½-inch cookies.

PEANUT BUTTER COOKIES

Mix ¾ cup peanut butter into butter-sugar mixture.

CHOCOLATE CHIP RAISIN COOKIES

Add 1 cup seedless raisins with the chocolate chips.

HOLIDAY FRUIT COOKIES

In place of chocolate chips, use 1 cup finely cut, mixed candied fruit.

Pictured opposite
Cereal 'N Chocolate Chip Cookies

Here's what's cookin' *Cereal 'n Chocolate Chip Cookies*
Recipe from the kitchen of **MRS. B**

1 3/4 C FLOUR	1/2 t SALT
1 t BAKING SODA	1 C BUTTER
3/4 C SUGAR	1 t VANILLA
3/4 C BROWN SUGAR	2 EGGS
2 C TOASTED RICE CEREAL	
1 6 OZ PKG CHOCOLATE CHIPS	

STIR TOGETHER FLOUR, SODA,
SET ASIDE. MEASURE

JELLY BEAN JOLLIES

½ c. butter
⅓ c. sugar
⅓ c. light brown sugar
 1 egg
½ t. baking soda
½ t. baking powder
½ t. salt
½ t. vanilla
1¼ c. flour
½ c. uncooked oats
 1 c. jelly beans or gumdrops, cut up

Cream together butter and sugars. Beat in egg, baking soda, baking powder, salt and vanilla. Stir in flour and oats until blended. Add jelly beans. Drop rounded spoonfuls of batter about 2 inches apart on lightly greased cookie sheet. Bake in 375° oven 10 to 12 minutes or until lightly browned. Makes 3 to 3½ dozen cookies.

The word "cereal" is kin to Ceres, the Roman goddess of vegetation.

RANGER COOKIES

½ c. shortening
½ c. granulated sugar
½ c. brown sugar
 1 egg
½ t. vanilla
 1 c. flour
½ t. baking soda
¼ t. baking powder
¼ t. salt
 1 c. uncooked oats
 1 c. whole wheat flakes
½ c. shredded coconut

Thoroughly mix shortening, sugars, egg and vanilla. Stir in remaining ingredients. Drop dough by rounded teaspoons 2 inches apart onto ungreased baking sheet. Bake in 375° oven 10 minutes. Immediately remove from baking sheet. Makes 3 dozen cookies, chewy on the inside, and crisp on the outside.

It's best to cool large cookies for one to two minutes before removing from the cookie sheet, unless the recipe directions tell you otherwise. That's because just-baked cookies are very tender and need the time to firm a bit before they're removed with a wide metal spatula.

CHOCOLATE BRAN CRISPS

 2 c. flour
½ t. baking soda
½ t. salt
 1 c. butter or margarine
1½ c. sugar
 2 eggs
 1 t. vanilla
 1 c. whole bran cereal
 1 6-oz. pkg. semisweet chocolate chips

Sift together flour, soda and salt. Set aside. Beat butter and sugar until light and fluffy. Add eggs and vanilla, beating well. Stir in bran cereal and chocolate chips. Add sifted dry ingredients. Mix well. Drop by level tablespoons onto ungreased baking sheets. Bake in 375° oven about 12 minutes or until lightly browned. Makes about 5½ dozen crisp cookies.

HONEY OAT DROPS

¾ c. flour
¼ t. salt
¼ t. baking soda
¼ c. butter or margarine
⅓ c. honey
¼ c. sour cream
½ t. vanilla
½ c. uncooked oats
½ c. coarsely chopped walnuts
¼ c. pitted dates, chopped

Sift flour with salt and baking soda. Cream together butter and honey. Stir in sour cream and vanilla. Blend in flour mixture and oats. Stir in walnuts and dates. Drop by rounded tablespoons onto greased and floured cookie sheets. Bake just above oven center at 325° about 15 minutes, until lightly browned. Let stand a minute, then remove to wire racks to cool. Makes 1½ dozen.

HONEY CEREAL COOKIES

2 c. flour
1 t. baking soda
½ t. baking powder
½ t. salt
1 c. butter
½ c. brown sugar
¾ c. granulated sugar
½ c. honey
1 egg
2 c. crisp whole wheat flakes
2 c. crisp sweetened rice cereal
1 c. flaked coconut

Sift flour with soda, baking powder and salt. Cream butter and sugars; add honey, egg and the flour mixture. Add cereals and coconut; mix thoroughly. Drop from teaspoon onto ungreased baking sheets. Bake at 375° for 8 to 10 minutes, or until golden brown. Let stand a few seconds before removing from baking sheet. (Cookies will become crisp when cool.) Makes about 8 dozen.

BANANA GRANOLA COOKIES

⅓ c. shortening
½ c. sugar
¼ c. molasses
1 egg
1⅓ c. ripe bananas, mashed (4 medium)
¼ c. nonfat dry milk powder
1¼ c. flour
1 t. baking powder
½ t. salt
¼ t. baking soda
⅛ t. ginger
½ t. grated lemon rind
½ c. flaked coconut
2 T. sesame seeds
¾ c. raisins
1 c. uncooked oats

In large mixing bowl, cream shortening and sugar. Beat in molasses and egg. Stir in bananas and dry milk powder. Sift together flour, baking powder, salt, baking soda and ginger; blend into batter. Stir in lemon rind, coconut, sesame seeds, raisins and oats. Drop by teaspoons onto greased baking sheets. Bake in 400° oven 10 minutes. Remove to rack and cool. Makes 4 dozen.

CHOCOLATE SNOW DROPS

1 c. flour
1 t. baking powder
¼ t. baking soda
¼ t. salt
½ c. coarsely chopped nuts
⅓ c. butter or margarine
1 c. brown sugar
1 egg
2 1-oz. squares unsweetened chocolate, melted
½ c. whole bran cereal
½ c. buttermilk or sour milk
½ t. vanilla flavoring

Sift together flour, baking powder, soda and salt; stir in nuts. Set aside. Cream together butter and sugar. Add egg and melted chocolate; mix thoroughly. Stir in bran cereal, buttermilk and vanilla. Add sifted dry ingredients; mix until combined. Drop by level tablespoons onto lightly greased baking sheets. (A walnut half can be gently pressed into top of each cookie.) Bake in 375° oven about 12 minutes or until cookie springs back when lightly touched. Remove immediately from baking sheets; cool on wire racks. Top cookies with confectioners' sugar frosting if desired. Makes about 3½ dozen 2¼-inch cookies.

CHOCOLATE WHEAT GERM BUTTERBALLS

¾ c. toasted wheat germ
¾ c. sugar
2 1-oz. squares semisweet chocolate
2 T. milk
1 c. butter
1½ t. vanilla
2½ c. flour
¼ t. salt
⅓ c. diced roasted almonds

Combine 1 tablespoon EACH of the wheat germ and sugar; reserve for coating. Melt chocolate and milk over low heat. Beat together butter and sugar. Stir in vanilla and melted chocolate. Gradually add flour mixed with salt and wheat germ. Mix in almonds. Shape dough into 48 balls. Dip into sugar and wheat germ. Place on ungreased baking sheet. Bake in 375° oven 11 to 12 minutes. Cool on rack. Makes 4 dozen.

GLAZED WHEAT GERM FLORENTINES

¼ c. shortening
⅔ c. toasted wheat germ
½ c. sugar
¼ c. flour
¼ t. salt
3 T. whipping cream
1 t. vanilla
¼ c. finely chopped almonds
3 1-oz. squares semisweet chocolate, melted

Melt shortening. Mix in all ingredients except chocolate. Drop teaspoon measures of mixture onto lightly greased baking sheet. Flatten with back of spoon. Bake in 350° oven 7 to 8 minutes or until lightly browned. Cool on baking sheet 2 minutes. Carefully remove and cool on racks. Spread bottoms of cooled cookies with melted chocolate. Store between layers of waxed paper. Makes about 3 dozen cookies.

TOASTED WHEAT GERM VIENNA BARS

2 eggs, separated
½ c. sugar
6 T. butter
2 t. grated lemon peel
1 t. vanilla
1¼ c. flour
¼ t. salt
¾ c. toasted wheat germ
¼ c. finely chopped walnuts
½ c. apricot jam
  Confectioners' sugar

Beat egg yolks with ¼ cup sugar. Beat in butter, lemon peel, vanilla, flour, salt and ½ cup wheat germ. Spread dough on greased baking sheet into 10 x 5-inch rectangle. Build up edges about ½ inch. Bake in 350° oven 12 to 15 minutes. Meanwhile, beat egg whites until foamy. Add remaining ¼ cup sugar gradually and beat until stiff. Fold in walnuts and remaining ¼ cup wheat germ. Spread jam over hot crust. Spread egg mixture on top. Return to oven and continue baking 15 to 18 minutes longer or until golden brown on top. Cool. Dust with confectioners' sugar. Cut into small bars. Makes about 3 dozen bars.

SOUR CREAM OATMEAL COOKIES

¾ c. butter
2 c. brown sugar
2 eggs, beaten
¾ c. sour cream
1 t. vanilla
2 c. flour
1 t. baking soda
2 c. uncooked oats
½ t. salt
½ t. cinnamon
1 c. raisins
½ c. chopped nuts

Cream butter and sugar until fluffy. Add eggs, sour cream and vanilla. Beat well. Sift together flour, soda, salt and cinnamon and add alternately with oats, nuts, and raisins. Beat until smooth. Drop by teaspoons on a greased cookie sheet. Bake at 350° about 15 minutes or until cookies are lightly browned and firm to touch. Cool on rack. Makes about 4½ dozen.

LUSCIOUS APRICOT BARS

⅔ c. dried apricots, finely chopped, or
¾ c. finely chopped prunes
½ c. butter or margarine
¼ c. granulated sugar
1 c. flour
½ c. whole bran cereal
½ t. baking powder
¼ t. salt
1 c. brown sugar
2 eggs
½ t. vanilla
½ c. finely chopped nuts
  Confectioners' sugar

Rinse apricots; place in small mixing bowl. Cover with very hot water and let stand 10 minutes or until fruit is tender. Drain well. Set aside. For crust, measure butter, granulated sugar and ½ cup flour into small mixing bowl; beat until smooth and creamy. Mix in bran cereal. Spread mixture evenly in bottom of ungreased 8 x 8 x 2-inch baking pan. Bake in 350° oven about 25 minutes or until lightly browned. Remove from oven; cool slightly. While crust is baking, sift together the remaining ½ cup flour, baking powder and salt. Set aside. Place brown sugar and eggs in large mixing bowl; beat well. Add sifted dry ingredients, vanilla, nuts and apricots; mix well. Spread mixture over baked crust. Return to 350° oven; bake 50 minutes or until lightly browned. Cool. Cut into bars. Roll in confectioners' sugar. Makes 32 bars.

PRIZE BROWNIES

Brownie lovers come in all sizes and ages. Some prefer a rich, moist, fudgy brownie. Others favor a nutty, frosting-covered cake-like bar.

In fact, some claim that the original brownie resulted from a disaster when an inventive baker rescued a fallen chocolate cake.

CHARLIE'S BROWNIES

1¼ c. flour
1 c. sugar
1 c. brown sugar
1 t. baking powder
1 t. salt
1 t. vanilla
½ c. butter, softened
¼ c. shortening
4 eggs
3 1-oz. envelopes pre-melted unsweetened chocolate
½ c. chopped nuts (optional)

Combine all ingredients in large mixing bowl. Beat at medium speed for 1 minute. Spread in greased 15 x 10-inch pan. Bake in preheated 350° oven for 25 to 30 minutes. Cool and frost. For thicker brownies, bake in a greased 13 x 9-inch pan for 30 to 35 minutes.

CHOCOLATE ICING

3 T. butter
3 T. milk
1 1-oz. envelope pre-melted unsweetened chocolate
2½ c. confectioners' sugar

Melt butter, milk and chocolate. Stir in sugar; beat until smooth. Spread on cooled brownies.

GROWN-UP BROWNIES

COOKIE BASE

½ c. brown sugar
¼ c. butter or margarine
¾ c. flour
¼ t. baking powder

Cream brown sugar and butter. Sift flour and baking powder and blend into sugar and butter mixture. Press into a greased 8- or 9-inch square pan. Bake at 350° for 10 minutes.

TOPPING

1¼ c. sugar
2 eggs
⅓ c. butter or margarine, melted
2 1-oz. envelopes pre-melted or
2 1-oz. squares unsweetened chocolate, melted
⅔ c. flour
½ t. baking powder
¼ t. salt
½ c. chopped nuts

Combine sugar and eggs; beat well. Stir in melted butter and chocolate. Sift together and blend in flour, baking powder and salt. Stir in chopped nuts. Spread Topping over partially baked cookie base. Bake at 350° for 25 minutes if using 9-inch pan; 35 minutes for 8-inch pan. Cool before cutting into squares. Makes 3 dozen 1½-inch squares.

GRAHAM CRACKER BROWNIES

½ c. brown sugar
½ c. granulated sugar
½ t. salt
1 t. vanilla
1 c. graham cracker crumbs
¾ c. raisins
⅓ c. chopped walnuts
2 eggs, beaten

Combine sugars, salt, vanilla, graham cracker crumbs, raisins and nuts. Add to beaten eggs and mix well. Spread evenly in greased and floured 8-inch square pan. Bake in a 350° oven for 25 minutes. Cool slightly; then turn out and cut into squares. Dust with confectioners' sugar, if desired. Makes 16 squares.

CHOCOLATE PEPPERMINT BROWNIES

4 1-oz. squares unsweetened chocolate
½ c. butter
2 c. sugar
4 eggs, beaten
1 c. flour
1 t. vanilla
1 c. coarsely chopped walnuts
15 to 20 chocolate peppermint patties

Melt chocolate and butter together over hot water. Cool slightly. Gradually add sugar and eggs, beating thoroughly after each addition. Blend in chocolate mixture. Stir in flour. Then add vanilla and nuts. Spread in greased 9-inch square pan. Bake in 325° oven about 40 minutes. Arrange chocolate peppermint patties over top of hot brownies; return to oven about 3 minutes to soften patties. Then spread to cover entire top of the brownies. Cool and cut into bars. Makes about 2 dozen brownies.

It's best to shell walnuts and keep the kernels refrigerated in airtight containers. Kept fresh, kernels break with a snap, taste crisp and clean.

WALNUT BROWNIES

⅓ c. shortening
1 6-oz. pkg. semisweet chocolate chips
¾ c. cake flour
½ c. sugar
½ t. baking powder
¼ t. salt
2 eggs
1 t. vanilla
1 c. coarsely chopped walnuts

Combine shortening and chocolate chips and melt over hot water. Cool slightly. Meanwhile, sift flour with sugar, baking powder and salt. Combine chocolate mixture, eggs and vanilla. Add dry ingredients and mix until smooth. Stir in walnuts. Spread into greased 8-inch square pan. Bake at 350° for about 30 minutes, just until top feels firm to touch. Cool in pan. Cut into squares or bars. Makes 15 brownies.

BUTTERSCOTCH BROWNIES

¼ c. butter
½ c. evaporated milk
2 c. light brown sugar
2 eggs, slightly beaten
½ t. salt
1½ c. flour
2 t. baking powder
1 t. vanilla
1 c. chopped pecans

In saucepan melt butter; remove from heat. Add evaporated milk, sugar, eggs and salt. Stir until well blended. Sift together flour and baking powder. Stir into egg mixture. Add vanilla and pecans. Spread evenly in greased 13 x 9-inch pan. Bake at 350° for 30 to 35 minutes. Cool in pan on wire rack. Cut into rectangles. Makes 3 dozen brownies.

PEANUT SWIRL BROWNIES

1 6-oz. pkg. semisweet chocolate chips
6 T. butter or margarine
⅓ c. honey
2 eggs, beaten
1 t. vanilla extract
½ c. flour
½ t. baking powder
1 c. peanut butter
½ c. sugar
½ c. milk
1 egg
   Dash of salt
½ c. chopped peanuts

Lightly grease a 9 x 9 x 2-inch baking pan. In a saucepan, over low heat, melt chocolate chips and butter, stirring constantly; cool. Gradually add honey to 2 beaten eggs. Blend in cooled chocolate mixture and vanilla. Stir together flour and baking powder. Add to chocolate mixture and stir just until dry ingredients are moistened. Pour half (1 cup) of brownie mixture into a lightly greased baking pan. Bake in a preheated 350° oven for 10 minutes. Blend peanut butter with sugar and beat in milk, egg and salt. Stir in nuts. Pour peanut mixture over partially baked brownie layer. Carefully spoon remaining brownie batter over peanut layer. Swirl slightly. Bake in a 350° oven about 30 to 35 minutes or until done. Makes about 24 bars.

RICH CHOCOLATE COOKIES

CHOCOLATE THUMBPRINTS

1 1-oz. square unsweetened chocolate
½ c. butter or margarine
½ c. sugar
1 egg, separated
¼ t. vanilla
1 c. flour
¼ t. salt
¾ c. finely chopped nuts
1 6-oz. pkg. semisweet chocolate chips

Melt chocolate over hot, not boiling, water. Cool slightly. Cream butter; add melted chocolate. Add sugar, egg yolk and vanilla and mix thoroughly. Sift together flour and salt. Add to chocolate mixture. Slightly beat egg white with fork. Roll dough into balls (about 1 teaspoon per ball); and dip balls in egg white to coat. Roll in nuts. Place about 1 inch apart on ungreased cookie sheet; press thumb gently in center of each. Bake in preheated 350° oven 10 to 12 minutes or until set. Transfer to cake rack. Immediately place 3 or 4 chocolates chips in the "thumbprint." When the chips have melted, spread evenly over the thumbprint. Makes about 3 dozen cookies.

The story of the cocoa bean is a romantic one. It could be labeled "the little brown bean that made good." Spaniards recognized the possibilities of chocolate, but kept it a secret for nearly one hundred years.

As late as the Eighteenth century, some Latin American growers ate only the slightly sweet flesh of the cocoa pod. They considered the bean a waste or, following the example of the Aztecs and Mayans, used it as currency.

CHOCOLATE COFFEE DROPS

2¼ c. flour
1 T. baking powder
1 t. salt
2 t. nutmeg
2 t. cinnamon
2 T. boiling water
2 T. instant coffee
⅔ c. shortening
1 c. dark brown sugar
1 egg
1 t. vanilla
1 12-oz. pkg. mini-chocolate chips
½ c. chopped nuts

Stir together flour, baking powder, salt, nutmeg and cinnamon and set aside. In small bowl, pour boiling water over coffee. Let cool. Cream shortening and sugar until light and fluffy. Beat in egg and vanilla. Add flour alternately with coffee. Stir in chocolate chips and nuts. Drop by level tablespoons on greased cookie sheet. Bake in preheated 375° oven 6 to 8 minutes. Makes about 4½ dozen.

CHOCOLATE BANANA COOKIES

3 c. flour
4½ t. baking powder
1½ t. salt
1 t. baking soda
1 c. butter
¾ c. sugar
½ c. light brown sugar
1 t. vanilla extract
1 egg
1 c. mashed banana
2 1-oz. squares semisweet or unsweetened chocolate, melted
1 c. chopped nuts
Confectioners' sugar

Sift together flour, baking powder, salt and soda. Cream together butter and sugars. Beat in vanilla and egg. Blend in banana, cooled chocolate and nuts. Stir in flour mixture. Drop by level tablespoons onto greased baking sheets. Bake in preheated 350° oven 12 to 14 minutes. Cool on wire racks. Sprinkle with confectioners' sugar. Makes about 6½ dozen.

SUGAR AND SPICE COOKIES

CRACKLE-TOP MOLASSES COOKIES

1 c. shortening	2 t. baking soda
2 c. brown sugar	2 t. dry mustard
1 egg, well beaten	1 t. vanilla
1 c. molasses	1 t. lemon extract
4 c. flour	Sugar
½ t. salt	

Cream shortening; add brown sugar. Blend in egg and molasses. Beat until light and fluffy. Sift dry ingredients; gradually blend into creamed mixture. (Dough should be soft but not sticky.) Add vanilla and lemon extract. Shape into 1-inch balls and place on a greased baking sheet. (Do not flatten.) Bake at 350° for 12 to 15 minutes, or until brown. Sprinkle with sugar; remove from baking sheet. Makes about 5 dozen.

PEANUT BUTTER HONEY SLICES

4 c. flour
1 t. baking soda
½ t. salt
1 t. cinnamon
1 c. smooth peanut butter
½ c. butter
½ c. sugar
1 c. honey
2 t. vanilla
2 eggs, well beaten

Sift together flour, soda, salt and cinnamon. Set aside. Cream peanut butter and butter. Add sugar, honey and vanilla and beat until fluffy. Add eggs. Stir in flour mixture. Shape into four 8-inch rolls. Wrap in waxed paper. Chill. Cut into ⅛-inch slices. Bake in 400° oven 5 to 8 minutes. Makes 6 dozen.

ORANGE SUGAR COOKIES

½ c. butter
½ c. sugar
2 eggs
1 T. orange juice concentrate, thawed
1 T. grated orange rind
2 c. flour
2 t. baking powder
½ c. sugar mixed with 2 T. grated orange rind

Cream butter and sugar. Beat in eggs, one at a time. Blend in undiluted orange concentrate and 1 tablespoon orange rind. Sift together flour and baking powder and blend into creamed mixture. Wrap in waxed paper and refrigerate 3 hours. Roll out on lightly floured surface to ¼-inch thickness. Cut with a 2-inch cookie cutter. Place on greased baking sheet and sprinkle with sugar mixed with orange rind. Bake in 375° oven for 8 to 10 minutes. Makes 5 dozen cookies.

Cool cookie sheets before placing rolled cookie dough on to bake. If cookie sheet is warm when cookies are placed on, they will have a bubbly appearance when baked.

GINGER HONEY BARS

2 c. cake flour
1¼ c. sugar
1 t. nutmeg
¼ t. baking soda
¼ t. salt
½ c. butter, melted
½ c. honey
4 egg whites
2 T. milk
½ c. crystallized ginger, diced

Sift flour with sugar, nutmeg, soda and salt. Add butter, honey, egg whites and milk, stirring until blended. Fold in crystallized ginger. Turn batter into two well greased and waxed paper lined 8 x 8 x 2-inch pans. Bake in 350° oven 35 minutes or until top is firm when pressed lightly. Turn out onto wire racks. Remove paper at once. Cool. Cut each cake into 24 squares. Store in a tightly covered container at least 2 to 3 days before serving. Flavor and texture improves with age. Makes 48 squares.

TULIP COOKIES

¾ c. sugar
½ c. butter
1 egg
1 egg yolk
1 t. grated orange rind
2 T. orange juice
2¼ c. flour
1 T. baking powder
1 t. salt
Glaze

Cream sugar and butter until light and fluffy. Blend in egg and egg yolk (reserving white for Glaze), orange rind and juice. Sift together dry ingredients. Gradually add to creamed mixture, blending thoroughly. Divide dough into 2 portions and chill 1 hour in refrigerator or 15 minutes in freezer. Roll out on lightly floured surface to 1/16-inch thickness. Cut circles with 4-inch round cookie cutter. Cut 3 petals from each circle, using about ⅓ of edge of cookie cutter. Arrange 3 petals in tulip shape for each cookie on lightly greased baking sheet. Bake in preheated 375° oven 5 to 6 minutes or until just golden at edges. Cool on racks. Spread with Glaze. Makes 3 dozen cookies.

GLAZE

1 egg white
1½ c. confectioners' sugar
1½ T. orange juice
    Yellow food coloring
    Red food coloring

Beat egg white until foamy. Blend in sugar and orange juice. If necessary, add more orange juice to make a thin glaze. Tint half of glaze pink and half yellow.

In Colonial times when sugar was scarce, or not available at all, molasses was used as the sweetener. Shipped in huge barrels from the West Indies, it was often called "long sweetening" whereas sugar was referred to as "short sweetening."

Today, molasses is still a popular ingredient, but most molasses cookie recipes call for a combination of molasses and sugar.

BROWN-EYED SUSANS

1 c. butter
1 c. confectioners' sugar
1 egg
1½ t. orange extract
2½ c. flour
1 t. salt
    Glaze

Cream butter; add sugar gradually. Beat in egg and extract. Blend in dry ingredients. Chill. Roll dough ¼ inch thick on floured surface. Cut with large and small daisy cutters. Place on ungreased cookie sheets. Bake at 375° about 10 minutes, depending on size. Make Glaze.

GLAZE

1 c. confectioners' sugar
2 T. milk
½ t. orange extract
    Yellow food coloring
    Cocoa

Combine sugar, milk and orange extract. Use several drops of food coloring to tint mixture a pale yellow. Brush warm cookies with the glaze. Add a small amount of cocoa and additional confectioners' sugar to remaining glaze to make dark chocolate frosting. Place ¼ teaspoonful frosting on center of large daisy cookie. Top with small daisy cookie. Decorate with bit of frosting. Makes 2½ dozen cookies.

CINNAMON CRISPS

1 c. butter or margarine
1 c. extra fine granulated sugar
1 egg, beaten
2½ c. flour
½ t. salt
2¼ t. cinnamon
1 c. coarsely chopped blanched almonds

Cream butter and sugar until light and fluffy. Add egg and mix well. Sift together dry ingredients and add to creamed mixture. Stir in chopped almonds. Mix well. Form into rolls 1½ inches in diameter. Wrap in waxed paper and place in refrigerator overnight. Slice ¼ inch thick. Bake on greased cookie sheets in a 350° oven 12 to 15 minutes. Makes 3½ dozen.

FAMILY FAVORITES

PINEAPPLE-FILLED COOKIES

1 c. butter
½ c. sugar
½ c. confectioners' sugar
1 egg
1½ t. vanilla
2¾ c. flour
¼ t. salt
½ t. baking soda
½ t. cream of tartar

Cream butter; add sugars gradually. Beat in egg and vanilla. Blend in dry ingredients. Chill. Make Pineapple Filling.

PINEAPPLE FILLING

1 T. water
1 T. cornstarch
½ c. pineapple jam

Combine all ingredients in saucepan. Cook at low heat until thick and clear. Cool.

Roll dough ⅛ inch thick on floured surface; cut with 2-inch scalloped cutter. Place half of the cookies on lightly greased cookie sheets. Place ½ teaspoons of filling in center of each cookie. Cut small holes in centers of remaining cookies; place on top of filling, sandwich fashion. Press each scallop together lightly with tip of finger. Bake at 350° about 12 minutes. Makes about 5 dozen cookies.

Remove cookies from baking sheet with a spatula as soon as they come out of the oven.

MINCEMEAT COOKIES

1½ c. flour
1½ t. baking soda
¼ c. water
2 eggs
⅓ c. shortening
¾ c. brown sugar
¾ t. cinnamon
¼ t. nutmeg
½ t. salt
½ c. chopped nuts
½ c. dry mincemeat

Sift together flour and baking soda. Set aside. Put next 7 ingredients into blender and blend until smooth. Add nuts and mincemeat and blend another second. Pour blended mixture into flour and stir until mixed. Drop by teaspoons onto greased baking sheet. Bake at 375° for 10 minutes. Immediately place on a wire cooling rack. Makes about 4 dozen cookies.

WHIRLIGIGS

3 c. flour
1 t. salt
¾ t. baking soda
¾ c. butter
1½ c. sugar
1 egg
2 t. vanilla
3 T. water
2 1-oz. squares unsweetened chocolate
Hot milk

Sift together flour, salt and soda. Cream butter and sugar until fluffy. Add egg and vanilla. Blend well. Add sifted dry ingredients and water. Mix well. Divide dough in half. Add melted chocolate to half of the dough. Shape each piece of dough into 2 rolls about 2 inches in diameter. Wrap in waxed paper. Refrigerate overnight. Cut each roll lengthwise into 4 equal quarters. Brush cut sides with hot milk. Place 4 strips of alternating color together to form a round cookie. Press firmly together. (There will be alternating chocolate and yellow quarters in each roll.) Return to refrigerator to firm. Cut into ⅛-inch slices. Bake on greased cookie sheets at 325° for 8 to 10 minutes or until cookies are slightly golden at edges. Cool on racks. Makes 12 dozen 2-inch cookies.

Pictured opposite
Tulip Cookies, page 49
Brown-Eyed Susans, page 49

ALMOND BRITTLE BARS

1 c. butter or margarine
2 t. instant coffee
1 t. salt
¾ t. almond extract
1 c. sugar
2 c. flour
1 6-oz. pkg. semisweet chocolate chips
½ c. flaked coconut
½ c. finely chopped almonds

Beat together butter, coffee, salt and almond extract. Gradually add sugar, beating until light and fluffy. Stir in flour, chocolate chips and coconut. Press batter into ungreased 15½ x 10½ x 1-inch jelly roll pan. Sprinkle almonds over top. Bake in 375° oven 23 to 25 minutes or until golden brown. Set pan on rack; cut 2½ x 1½-inch bars while warm. When cool, remove from pan. Makes 40 bars.

Note: If you want to break the cookies in irregular pieces, cool baked cookie dough in pan on rack, then break it in pieces with your fingers. Cookies are crisp.

UNIQUE DATE COOKIES

1 c. sugar
1 c. brown sugar
1 c. butter
3 eggs
1 t. vanilla
4 c. flour
1 t. salt
1 t. baking soda
Filling

Cream butter and sugars until light. Add eggs and beat until light and fluffy. Mix in vanilla. Add sifted dry ingredients. Mix well. Chill dough. Roll out on lightly floured board and spread with filling. Roll up like jelly roll. Chill again overnight. Slice ⅛-inch thick and place on lightly greased baking sheets. Bake in 375° oven for 10 to 12 minutes or until lightly browned. Makes about 6 dozen cookies.

FILLING

1 lb. dates, finely chopped
½ c. sugar
½ c. water

Combine ingredients in saucepan. Bring to a boil over medium heat, stirring constantly. Boil 1 minute. Remove from heat and set aside to cool.

CHERRY COCONUT CHEWS

2 c. flour
½ t. baking powder
½ t. baking soda
½ t. salt
⅔ c. shortening
⅔ c. sugar
1 egg
½ c. milk
1 t. vanilla
1 c. flaked coconut
¼ c. maraschino cherries, chopped and drained

Sift flour, baking powder, soda and salt together. Set aside. In a large bowl, cream shortening with sugar until fluffy. Beat in egg, milk and vanilla. Stir in flour mixture until well blended. Stir in coconut and cherries. Drop by rounded teaspoonsful onto lightly greased cookie sheets. Bake in 375° oven 10 minutes or until firm and lightly golden around edges. Remove from cookie sheets to cool. Makes about 4½ dozen.

CHOCOLATE DATE JUMBLES

2 1-oz. squares unsweetened chocolate
½ c. shortening
1½ c. sugar
1 t. vanilla
2 eggs
1 c. sour cream
2¾ c. flour
½ t. baking soda
½ t. baking powder
1 t. salt
1 8-oz. pkg. pitted dates, cut up
1 c. chopped walnuts

Melt chocolate over hot water. Cool. Cream shortening and sugar until creamy; add vanilla and eggs and beat until fluffy. Stir in chocolate and sour cream. Sift together next four ingredients. Add with dates and nuts to sugar mixture. Blend well. Drop by teaspoons about 2 inches apart on greased cookie sheet. Bake in a 400° oven 8 to 10 minutes or until done. Remove to rack to cool. Makes 4½ dozen cookies.

COOKIES WITH A FOREIGN ACCENT

AMARETTI
(ITALIAN MACAROONS)

½ lb. ground blanched almonds
1 c. sugar
¼ t. salt
2 egg whites, stiffly beaten
½ t. almond extract
  Confectioners' sugar
  Colored sugar and decorators

Combine almonds, sugar, and salt; fold into beaten egg whites. Add almond extract. Drop by teaspoons (or roll into small balls) on greased and floured cookie sheets. Sprinkle with confectioners' sugar, then with colored sugar or decorators. Let stand 2 hours before baking. Bake at 300° about 20 to 25 minutes or until lightly browned. Makes about 3 dozen.

Some of the most enchanting concoctions to emerge from European kitchens are the delectable desserts baked in fanciful shapes. Austrians delight in the "Rebrucken," a chocolate frosted "saddle of venison"; whereas the German specialty is the "Igel," a cake resembling a hedgehog with raisins for eyes and split almonds for quills. In Lithuania, the favorite goodie is "Grybai," crisp, frosted cookies in the shape of plump mushrooms that look as if they had just been picked from a cool forest floor. Grybai in their charming mushroom shapes are traditional Lithuanian Christmas cookies.

Though easy to make, Grybai do take a little time and patience to frost. Bake a batch of Grybai in assorted sizes—some tiny buttons, others fat and sassy. Packaged in pretty flowerpots or straw baskets, they make charming and welcome gifts.

GRYBAI
(SPICED MUSHROOM COOKIES)

3 T. butter
¼ c. sugar
1 egg
½ c. honey, heated and cooled to lukewarm
2 c. flour
2 T. lemon-flavored instant tea
¾ t. baking soda
½ t. cinnamon
¼ t. cloves
¼ t. ginger
¼ t. nutmeg
  White Icing
  Chocolate Icing

In large bowl, blend butter and sugar; beat in egg and honey. Sift together dry ingredients. Gradually add to butter mixture, blending well. Wrap dough in waxed paper and chill at least 1 hour. Preheat oven to 350°. Shape ⅓ of the dough into mushroom-like stems ¼ inch in diameter and 1½ inches long. Shape remaining dough into an equal number of balls 1 inch in diameter. Indent 1 side of each ball with thumb to form a mushroom-like cap. Place balls rounded side up, laying stems separately on sides, on greased cookie sheets. Bake 10 minutes; cool on wire racks. Makes about 3 dozen cookies.

To assemble, dip end of stem into White Icing and fit into indentation of cap; allow icing to set. Coat stem and underside of cap with White Icing, then top cap with Chocolate Icing.

WHITE ICING

In small bowl, blend 2½ cups confectioners' sugar with 3 to 4 tablespoons milk.

CHOCOLATE ICING

In small bowl, blend 2 cups confectioners' sugar, 1 tablespoon cocoa and 2 to 3 tablespoons milk.

When cookies are cool and ready for storage, place in a cookie jar or can which has a tightly fitting cover. Store only one kind of cookie in each container.

GERMAN PFEFFERNUESSE

½ c. butter, melted
1 c. sugar
2 eggs
½ t. grated lemon rind
½ t. anise oil
2 c. flour
1½ t. cinnamon
½ t. cloves
½ t. baking soda
½ c. citron, finely chopped
1½ c. finely chopped blanched almonds
Confectioners' sugar

Combine melted butter, sugar and eggs. Blend well. Add lemon rind and anise oil. Sift together flour, cinnamon, cloves and soda. Add to butter mixture. Add citron and almonds. Blend. Shape into small balls, using 1 teaspoon of dough. Place on greased cookie sheets. Bake at 350° for 12 to 14 minutes. While warm roll in confectioners' sugar. Store in airtight container and allow to mellow 2 to 3 weeks. Makes about 15 dozen cookies.

NORWEGIAN BUTTER COOKIES

1 c. butter
½ c. sugar
2 hard-boiled egg yolks
2 raw egg yolks
2½ c. flour
1 egg white, slightly beaten
Granulated sugar

Cream butter and sugar until light and fluffy. Force hard-boiled egg yolks through a wire sieve. Add sieved egg yolks and raw egg yolks to creamed mixture, mixing thoroughly. Add flour and mix until smooth. Chill dough for several hours or overnight. Pinch off small balls of dough about ½- to ¾-inch diameter. Roll into strips 4 to 5 inches long and about the size of a lead pencil. Tie each strip into a knot. Place on lightly buttered cookie sheet. Brush with egg white and sprinkle with sugar. Bake in 350° oven 8 to 10 minutes or until lightly browned. Carefully remove from cookie sheet to avoid breaking and place on cooling rack. Makes 4 dozen cookies.

MEXICAN CINNAMON TEA CAKES

1¼ c. sugar
1 c. butter or margarine, softened
1½ t. cinnamon
¼ t. baking soda
2¾ c. flour

Cream the butter with 1 cup of the sugar, ½ teaspoon of the cinnamon and soda. Add flour. Roll on lightly floured board to ⅛-inch thickness. Shape with 1½-inch cookie cutters. Place on ungreased cookie sheets. Bake in a 400° oven 8 to 10 minutes or until cookies are lightly browned around edges. While still hot, combine remaining sugar and cinnamon and sprinkle over tops of cookies. Store in a tightly closed cookie jar. Makes 4½ dozen.

ENGLISH TEA LOGS

5⅓ c. flour
1½ c. butter or margarine
2 eggs
2 t. sugar
1 t. salt
1½ c. finely chopped apple
¾ c. raisins
3 T. sugar
1 T. lemon-flavored instant tea
1 t. cinnamon
Confectioners' sugar

Place flour in large bowl, making a well in center. Into the well, put butter, eggs, sugar and salt. Using the fingertips, make a paste of the center ingredients, gradually incorporating flour until a smooth, firm ball is formed. Wrap in waxed paper; refrigerate 2 to 3 hours. In small bowl, combine apples, raisins, sugar, lemon-flavored instant tea and cinnamon. Between lightly floured waxed paper, roll half the dough into an oblong, ⅛ inch thick. Cut dough into 2-inch squares. Place a teaspoon of filling in the center of each square. Roll square like a log and seal ends. Place on ungreased cookie sheet, seam side down. Repeat above procedure for other half of dough. Bake in 375° oven 20 minutes. Sift confectioners' sugar over logs while still hot. Makes about 5 dozen tea logs.

Kriskletts

KRISKLETTS
(MOROCCAN ANISE TIDBITS)

3 c. flour	1 T. anise seed,
1 c. sugar	crushed
3 t. baking powder	¾ c. water
½ t. salt	3 T. salad oil

Sift flour with sugar, baking powder and salt. Stir in anise seed. Add approximately ¾ cup water, a little at a time, mixing until dry ingredients are moistened (dough should be slightly rubbery.) Work oil into dough. Shape dough into pencil-thin rolls by rolling dough with the palms of your hands on a lightly floured board. Cut each roll into ½-inch pieces. Place on greased cookie sheets and bake in a 350° oven 15 to 20 minutes. Cool and store in a dry place. Serve with minted tea if desired. Makes about 1½ pounds.

COOKIE SPECTACULARS

TRI-CORNERED HATS

½ c. lemon-flavored instant tea
¾ c. butter or margarine, softened
1 egg
1 t. vanilla
2¾ c. flour
¼ c. milk
2¼ c. ready-to-use mincemeat
2 T. rum or ⅛ t. rum extract
Confectioners' sugar

Blend tea and butter until light and fluffy. Add egg and vanilla. Alternately stir in flour and milk, blending well. Chill 1 hour. On lightly floured board, roll ¼ of the dough at a time ⅛ inch thick. Cut with 3-inch round cookie cutters. Combine mincemeat and rum. Place ½ tablespoon mincemeat in center of each circle. Form hat by lifting edges up and pinching together tightly at 3 points equally distant from each other, leaving filling exposed. Bake on ungreased cookie sheets in 350° oven 10 to 12 minutes. Cool. If desired, pipe edges with softened cream cheese or sprinkle with confectioners' sugar. Makes about 4 dozen.

Austrian peach cookies are the inspiration of a clever Austrian baker.

The peach, held in high esteem since the Middle Ages, is often called the "gold that grows on trees." Some believe the peach originated in China 3,000 years ago. The peach reached the New World in the fifteenth century.

This richly decorated little peach confection is a delightful gift to bake for a friend or serve for a special luncheon.

AUSTRIAN PEACH COOKIES

1 c. sugar
¾ c. vegetable oil
½ c. milk
2 eggs
¾ t. baking powder
½ t. vanilla
3½ to 4 c. flour
Apricot filling
Red and Yellow-Orange Sugars

In large bowl, combine sugar, oil, milk, eggs, baking powder and vanilla. Blend in enough flour to form a soft dough. Roll into walnut-size balls and bake on ungreased cookie sheets in 325° oven 15 to 20 minutes (cookies will be pale). Cool completely. Scrape out cookies by gently rotating tip of sharp knife against flat side of cookie, leaving shell and reserving crumbs. Fill cookies with apricot filling. Press two cookies together to form a "peach." Brush lightly with additional brandy or water and immediately dip one spot in Red Sugar for blush, then roll entire cookie in Yellow-Orange Sugar for peach color. If desired, insert a piece of cinnamon stick "stem" through green gumdrop "leaf" into the stem of each peach. Makes 2½ dozen.

APRICOT FILLING

2 c. reserved cookie crumbs
1 c. peach or apricot preserves
½ c. chopped almonds
1 3-oz. pkg. cream cheese, softened
2 T. instant tea
2 to 3 T. peach, apricot or plain brandy
¾ t. ground cinnamon

In medium bowl combine 2 cups reserved crumbs, preserves, almonds, cream cheese, instant tea powder, brandy and cinnamon.

RED AND YELLOW-ORANGE SUGARS

1 c. sugar
Red food coloring
Yellow food coloring

To make red sugar: blend ⅓ cup sugar with a few drops of red food coloring. To make yellow-orange sugar: blend ⅔ cup sugar with 2 to 3 drops red food coloring and enough yellow food coloring to make a peach color.

FORTUNE TEA COOKIES

3 egg whites
¾ c. sugar
⅛ t. salt
½ c. butter or margarine, melted
¼ t. vanilla
1 c. flour
1 T. instant tea
2 T. water
   Freezer paper cut in 2 x 2½-inch strips
   with fortunes written on them

In medium bowl, combine egg whites, sugar and salt. Stir in thoroughly, one at a time, butter, vanilla, flour, tea and water. Chill at least 20 minutes. Make only 2 cookies at a time. On greased baking sheet, drop 2 slightly rounded teaspoonsful of dough 4 inches apart. Spread dough very thin with back of spoon to about 3 inches in diameter. Bake in 350° oven 5 minutes or until edges turn lightly brown. Remove immediately to wire rack. Cookies should be paper thin. Working quickly, place one fortune in center of each cookie. Fold cookie in half, enclosing fortune, to form a semicircle. Grasp rounded edges of semicircle between thumb and forefinger of one hand. At center of folded edge, push in with forefinger of other hand. Solid sides of cookie will puff out. Keeping forefinger in place, bring edges of fold downward around forefinger. Place each cookie in small-size muffin tin, open edges up, until cookie sets. Store in airtight container. Makes about 4 dozen cookies.

The ever popular Chinese fortune cookie appears to be inspired by the West. It is unlikely that you will find a recipe for it in an authentic Chinese cookbook.

According to one legend, fortune cookies were created in a moment of inspiration by a Japanese chef in San Francisco. Ironically, these whimsies with fortune slips have become a standard and fascinating end to many Oriental meals.

No newcomer to the snack scene, pretzels may once have been a symbol of the solar cycle and date back to Roman times. No one really knows who baked the first pretzel or twisted it into a circular shape.

Some legends claim, however, that a monk in the monastery bakery twisted bread scraps into a circle, twisting the ends to symbolize arms crossed in prayer. Priests later used pretzels to reward students for learning their prayers. These twisted shapes were called *pretiola*, Latin for small reward.

Pretzels eventually became a holy symbol of prayer and penance. Later, they were known by still another Latin name, *bracellae*, which means little arms. By the fifth century, pretzels were a popular Christian Lenten bread. Since the original pretzel recipes did not call for eggs, shortening, or milk, the flour, water and salt product was acceptable to eat during Lent.

Today pretzels, salted or plain, come in all sizes and shapes: long and short, thick and thin, nuggets, and the familiar ring with crossed ends.

PRETZEL COOKIES

¾ c. butter
½ c. sugar
1 t. vanilla
1¾ c. flour
2 T. milk
1 egg, slightly beaten
   Colored sugar

Cream butter, sugar and vanilla until light and fluffy. Gradually add flour and milk, mixing until well blended. Chill dough for ease in handling. Divide dough into 4 equal parts. Work with one part of dough at a time, refrigerating remaining dough. Divide each part into 8 pieces. Roll each piece between hands to form an 8-inch strand. Place on cookie sheet, twisting into pretzel shape. Brush dough with egg and sprinkle with sugar. Bake in preheated 400° oven 8 to 10 minutes or until lightly browned. Remove to wire racks to cool. Makes 32 pretzel cookies.

HOLIDAY COOKIES

CHOCOLATE SUGAR PUFFS

½ c. salad oil
4 1-oz. squares unsweetened chocolate
2 c. sugar
4 eggs, beaten
2 t. vanilla
2½ c. flour
2 t. baking powder
½ t. salt
½ c. chopped walnuts or pecans (optional)
1 c. confectioners' sugar

Combine oil, melted chocolate and sugar. Stir in eggs and vanilla. Sift together flour, baking powder and salt; add to sugar mixture. Stir in nuts. Chill dough 2 to 4 hours or overnight. Shape dough into small balls, about ¾ inch in diameter. Roll in confectioners' sugar. Place on lightly greased cookie sheets. Bake at 350° for 10 to 12 minutes. Makes about 6 dozen cookies.

SANTA'S WHISKERS

1 c. butter or margarine
1 c. sugar
1 t. almond extract
2½ c. flour
¾ c. maraschino cherries, finely chopped
½ c. finely chopped pecans
¾ c. flaked coconut

Cream butter and sugar, blend in extract. Stir in flour, cherries and nuts. Form in 2 rolls, each 2 inches in diameter and 8 inches long. Roll in coconut. Wrap and chill several hours or overnight. Slice ¼ inch thick; place on ungreased cookie sheet. Bake at 375° for 12 minutes or until edges are golden. Makes 5 dozen.

BON BON COOKIES

1 c. dates, finely ground
½ c. finely ground walnuts
½ t. vanilla
2 egg whites
⅛ t. salt
⅔ c. sugar
½ t. vanilla
Red food coloring
Green food coloring

Combine dates, nuts and vanilla. Shape into small balls using ½ teaspoon of mixture. Beat egg whites and salt until stiff but not dry. Add sugar gradually. Beat until mixture holds a firm peak. Add vanilla. Blend. Divide meringue in half. Tint one half green and the other pink. Drop balls into meringue. Cover with meringue. Remove each ball with a teaspoon. Place on greased cookie sheet. Swirl top. Bake at 250° about 30 minutes. Makes about 4 dozen cookies.

HOLIDAY FRUIT DROPS

1 c. shortening
2 c. brown sugar
2 eggs
½ c. buttermilk
3½ c. flour
1 t. baking soda
1 t. salt
1½ c. pecan pieces
2 c. candied cherries, halved
2 c. dates, cut up

Mix shortening, sugar and eggs. Stir in buttermilk. Sift dry ingredients. Stir into shortening mixture. Fold in pecans, cherries and dates. Chill at least 1 hour. Drop rounded teaspoons of dough about 2 inches apart on lightly greased baking sheet. Place a pecan half on each cookie, if desired. Bake in 400° oven 8 to 10 minutes, until almost no imprint remains when touched lightly. Holiday Fruit Drops improve with storing. Makes about 8 dozen.

> Avoid working in too much flour in rolled cookies. Chill dough thoroughly before rolling.

ROLLED SPICED CHRISTMAS COOKIES

4 c. flour
1¾ c. sugar
1 t. allspice
1 t. cinnamon
1½ c. butter or margarine
2 eggs, lightly beaten
3 T. cold water

Sift together first 4 ingredients. Cut in butter until mixture resembles coarse meal. Stir in eggs and water, mixing well. (Dough will be stiff but do not add more water.) Chill until dough can be handled easily, about 1 hour. Roll to ⅛-inch thickness on a lightly floured board. Shape with assorted cookie cutters. Bake on ungreased cookie sheets in a 400° oven 7 to 8 minutes or until lightly browned around the edges. Cool on wire racks. Frost as desired with confectioners' sugar icing. Decorate with colored sugar, cinnamon drops and bits of candied fruits. Makes about 9 dozen cookies of assorted shapes and sizes.

GINGERBREAD MEN

4 c. flour
1 T. ginger
1 t. baking soda
1 t. salt
1 t. cinnamon
1 c. butter, softened
1 c. light brown sugar
½ c. light molasses

Sift together dry ingredients and set aside. Cream butter and sugar until light and fluffy. Blend in molasses. Gradually add flour mixture. Mix thoroughly. Chill until firm, 1 to 2 hours. Divide dough into quarters. On large ungreased baking sheets roll each quarter out to ⅛-inch thickness. Cut with 5-inch tall gingerbread man cutter. Remove dough between cookie cutouts; re-roll excess dough on another baking sheet. Bake cookies in a 375° oven 7 to 8 minutes, or until lightly browned. Cool slightly before removing from baking sheets. Cool completely; decorate as desired. Makes 4 to 5 dozen.

Giving gifts of Christmas cookies is not a new idea or even entirely American.

According to an old Danish legend, no Christmas visitor is allowed to leave the house without taking a bag of Christmas cookies. Otherwise the host and hostess run the risk of the holiday visitor carrying the Christmas Spirit away in his empty hands.

MARZIPAN BARS

½ c. butter
½ c. brown sugar
1 egg yolk
1 t. vanilla
½ t. baking soda
2 c. flour
¼ t. salt
¼ c. milk
1 c. red raspberry jelly

Cream butter and sugar. Beat in egg yolk and vanilla. Sift together flour, soda and salt. Add dry ingredients and milk. Spread onto bottom of greased 10 x 15 x 1-inch pan; cover with jelly. Make filling.

ALMOND PASTE FILLING

1 8-oz. can almond paste, cut in small pieces
1 egg white
½ c. sugar
1 t. vanilla
3 T. butter
3 eggs
Green food coloring

Blend almond paste, egg white, sugar, vanilla and butter until smooth. Add eggs one at a time and beat well. Tint mixture a delicate green; pour over jelly layer. Bake at 350° for 35 to 40 minutes. Cool. Make icing.

CHOCOLATE ICING

2 1-oz. squares unsweetened chocolate, melted
1 T. butter
1 t. vanilla
2 c. confectioners' sugar
About ¼ c. hot milk

Combine all ingredients; beat until smooth. Spread over almond layer and cut into small bars.

CHEESECAKE COOKIES

1 c. butter, softened
1 c. sugar
½ t. vanilla or almond extract
2 c. self-rising flour
   Cream Cheese Topping
2 c. sliced almonds (optional)

Cream butter and sugar until light and fluffy. Stir in flavoring. Gradually add flour and mix well. Pat or spread dough evenly over bottom of ungreased 15½ x 10½ x 1-inch jelly roll pan. Bake in 350° oven 20 minutes or until lightly browned. Cool. Spread crust with Cream Cheese Topping. If desired, sprinkle top with almonds. Continue baking in 350° oven 30 to 35 minutes. Cool completely before cutting into bars. Makes 4 dozen.

CREAM CHEESE TOPPING

2 8-oz. pkgs. cream cheese, softened
2 eggs
½ t. vanilla or almond extract
½ c. confectioners' sugar
1 c. sour cream

Beat cream cheese until smooth. Add eggs and flavoring, beating until smooth. Stir in sugar. Fold in sour cream.

SNOWBALLS

¼ c. butter
4 c. miniature marshmallows
5 c. crisp rice cereal
1⅓ c. flaked coconut

Melt butter in large saucepan. Add marshmallows. Cook over low heat, stirring constantly, until marshmallows are melted and mixture is very syrupy. Remove from heat. Add rice cereal; stir until well coated. With buttered fingers, shape into 24 balls about 2 inches in diameter. Roll in coconut. Let stand until cool. Makes 24 2-inch Snowballs.
Note: To store Snowballs in freezer, wrap tightly or place in airtight container.

PEPPERMINT SNOWBALLS

Add ½ cup crushed hard peppermint candy with the rice cereal. For variety use other flavored hard candy.

PEANUT BUTTER CANES

½ c. margarine   1 egg
½ c. sugar   ½ t. vanilla
½ c. brown sugar   1¼ c. flour
1 c. creamy peanut   ½ t. salt
   butter   ½ t. baking soda

Cream margarine and sugars until fluffy. Beat in peanut butter, egg and vanilla. Add flour, salt and soda, blending well. For each cookie, shape 1 level tablespoon of dough into pencil shape about 6 inches long and ¼ inch thick. Shape in the form of a candy cane. Bake on ungreased baking sheets in 375° oven about 10 minutes or until done. Cool cookies on brown or other absorbent paper. When cool, decorate with red and white Confectioners' Sugar and Water Icing and sprinkle with colored sugar, if desired. Tie bow around stem of cane with red and green ribbon. Makes about 4 dozen.

When a cookie recipe calls for chopped candied fruit, dates, prunes, raisins or other dried fruit, it's easier to cut them with a kitchen shears rather than a knife.

POINSETTIA COOKIES

2 c. confectioners' sugar
1 c. butter or margarine
2 eggs
1 t. vanilla
½ t. rum extract
3 c. flour
1 t. salt
1 c. shredded coconut
1 c. butterscotch chips
   Granulated sugar
½ c. candied red cherries, cut in wedges

Beat together confectioners' sugar and butter. Add eggs and extracts. Sift together flour and salt and stir into butter mixture. Add coconut and ¾ cup of the butterscotch morsels. Chill dough until firm. Roll into 1-inch balls. Place on ungreased cookie sheets. Flatten cookie with bottom of glass dipped in granulated sugar. Place a butterscotch morsel in center of each cookie. Place cherry wedges in a circle to resemble a poinsettia. Bake at 375° about 12 minutes. Makes about 5 dozen.

INDEX

A very special thank you to the following for their cooperation and help: American Spice Trade Association; Banana Bunch; California Apricot Advisory Board; California Tree Fruit Agreement; California Raisin Advisory Board; Castle & Cooke Foods; Chocolate Manufacturers Association; Del Monte Corporation; Diamond Walnut Growers, Inc.; Florida Citrus Commission; General Foods; General Mills, Inc.; Glidden-Durkee; Great Western Sugar; Hershey Foods; International Multifoods; Kellogg Company; Libby, McNeill & Libby; National Cherry Growers & Industries Foundation; Nestle Company; Oklahoma Peanut Commission; Peanut Growers of Georgia & Alabama; Pillsbury Company; Quaker Oats Company; R. T. French Company; Standard Brands, Inc.; Stokely-Van Camp, Inc.; Sunkist Growers, Inc.; Sunsweet Growers, Inc.; Thomas J. Lipton, Inc.; United Dairy Industry Association; University of Wisconsin-Extension; Washington Apple Commission; Wheat Flour Institute.

Cover recipes:

Fabulous Filbert Bars, page 16
Whirligigs, page 50
Chocolate Sugar Puffs, page 59
Sour Cream Orange Cookies, page 11
German Walnut Cakes, page 33
Poinsettia Cookies, page 61
Austrian Peach Cookies, page 56

OTHER COOKBOOKS AVAILABLE

All Holidays Cookbook
American Cookbook
Barbecue Cookbook
Christmas Cookbook
Christmas Gifts from the Kitchen
Country Bread Cookbook
Country Kitchen
Family Cookbook
Farmhouse Cookbook
Festive Party Cookbook
Fish and Seafood Cookbook
From Mama's Honey Jar
Gourmet Appetizer Cookbook
Gourmet on the Go
Gourmet Touch
Guide to Microwave Cooking
Have a Gourmet Christmas
Junior Chef Cookbook
Meatless Meals Cookbook
Menus from Around the World
Naturally Nutritious
Nice and Easy Desserts
Simply Delicious
Soups for All Seasons
Tempting Treasures
Whole Grain Cookbook

A wide variety of cookie cutters in all shapes and sizes can be obtained from the following companies:

Maid of Scandinavia
3244 Raleigh Avenue
Minneapolis, Minnesota 55416

Educational Products Co.
Hope, New Jersey 07844

SX517 BOOK VIEWER STAND — *The modern see-through book stand, made of strong, durable Lucite, completely protects cookbooks and other display items from smudges and dirt. The stand conveniently folds flat for easy storage or hanging. It's perfect for use in the kitchen, workshop, or home-study. A great gift idea and it's only $4.00, plus $1.00 postage and handling. Price subject to change without notice.*

IDEALS RECIPE CARD BOOKLETS—*Each booklet contains 32 individual 3" x 5" recipe cards, perforated for easy removal. Booklets are available in two distinctive designs and each includes a delicious easy-to-make recipe. Ideals Recipe Card Booklets may be purchased for one dollar from your local bookstore.*